Columbia University

Contributions to Education

Teachers College Series

No. 305

AMS PRESS
NEW YORK

CONTROL OF AVAILABLE PUBLIC SCHOOL INCOME

WITH SPECIAL REFERENCE TO CITIES OF NEW YORK STATE

144821

By

DALE S. YOUNG, Ph.D.

DIRECTOR OF RESEARCH, STATE DEPARTMENT OF EDUCATION.
MONTGOMERY, ALABAMA

TEACHERS COLLEGE, COLUMBIA UNIVERSITY
CONTRIBUTIONS TO EDUCATION, NO. 305

LB2830
Y6
1972

BUREAU OF PUBLICATIONS
Teachers College, Columbia University
NEW YORK CITY
1928

Library of Congress Cataloging in Publication Data

Young, Dale S   1893-
    Control of available public school income.

    Reprint of the 1928 ed., issued in series: Teachers
College, Columbia University. Contributions to
education, no. 305.
    Originally presented as the author's thesis,
Columbia.
    Bibliography: p.
    1. Education--New York (State)--Finance.
I. Title. II. Series: Columbia University.
Teachers College. Contributions to education, no. 305

LB2830.Y6 1972   379'.13'09747   73-177614
ISBN 0-404-55305-2

Reprinted by Special Arrangement with Teachers
College Press, New York, New York

From the edition of 1928, New York
First AMS edition published in 1972
Manufactured in the United States

AMS PRESS, INC.
NEW YORK, N. Y.   10003

9.85

ACKNOWLEDGMENTS

The writer is indebted to many individuals for their coöperation during the investigation of this problem. He is chiefly under obligation to Doctors N. L. Engelhardt, Carter Alexander, and J. R. McGaughy, who, as members of his dissertation committee were of material assistance in formulating and carrying out the present study. To Doctor G. D. Strayer, Doctor P. R. Mort, and contemporary students in Educational Administration at Teachers College the writer wishes to express his appreciation for their continued interest and assistance.

Thanks are due the many local school and municipal officials who made available the data without which this study could not have been made. These officials, as well as state authorities in Albany, gave freely and cheerfully of their time in order to furnish needed facts.

Without the assistance of his wife, Mary Padou Young, the writer could not have completed this study at this time.

D. S. Y.

CONTENTS

CHAPTER   PAGE

I. THE PROBLEM... 1

Previous Studies in Finance.................................... 1
   Methods of Financial Control and Their Application to School
     Finance.. 1
The Present Study... 3
   Statement of the Problem.................................. 3
   Scope of the Study.. 4
   Sources of Data... 4
   Securing the Data... 4
     Fiscal Period for Which Data Were Secured................ 4
     School Systems Supplying the Data....................... 6
     Method by Which Data Were Secured..................... 6
     Other Data... 7
   Definition of Terms Used.................................. 7
     Public School Income.................................... 7
     Expenditure and Disbursement........................... 8
     Expense.. 8
     Income Control—External and Internal................... 8
   Bibliography.. 9

II. EXTERNAL INCOME CONTROL................................. 10

Introduction... 10
Present Status of the Cities Visited............................ 10
Trend Toward Fiscal Independence of School Boards............ 14
Budgetary Review.. 15
   Personnel... 15
Adoption of the Budget by the School Board and Its Submission
   for Review... 16
   Analysis of Tables IV, V, and VI........................... 16
   Time Consumed in Review.................................. 20
Summary.. 22

III. INTERNAL INCOME CONTROL................................. 24

Introduction... 24
The Budget.. 25
Preparation of the Budget..................................... 25
Items Not Included in the Budget.............................. 26
   Capital Outlay and Debt Service............................ 27
   Teachers' Retirement Fund................................. 28
     Present Method of Maintenance.......................... 28
     Hypothetical Sample Budgets............................ 31
     Present Practice in Budgeting for Teachers' Retirement Fund.. 32
     Recommendation for Collecting Contributions.............. 38

CHAPTER   PAGE

III. INTERNAL INCOME CONTROL (*continued*)
  Estimated Revenues.. 38
  Estimated Expenditures for Current Expense.................... 42
  Summary.. 43

IV. THE TAX CALENDAR AND THE FISCAL YEAR.................... 44
  Introduction.. 44
  School Tax Levy... 45
  School Tax Collection.. 47
    Collection Official... 47
    Combined Tax Collection................................... 49
      Changes During Ten-Year Period......................... 49
      Cities Grouped According to Combination................... 49
    Coördination of the Tax Calendar and the Fiscal Year........... 49
      The Situation in Cities in Other States...................... 49
      The Situation in Cities in New York State................... 51
      Technique Used for Comparisons.......................... 54
      Analysis of Data....................................... 55
      Submission and Testing of Hypotheses..................... 55
      Comparison of Cities in Tables XIX and XX................ 56
      Factors Accompanying Delayed Tax Collection.............. 62
      Further Analysis of Groupings............................ 62
      How to Interpret Tables XXI to XXVI..................... 63
      Analysis of Groupings Continued......................... 68
  The Fiscal Year and the Submission of the Annual School Estimate 74
  Technique Used... 74
  Application of Technique..................................... 74
    Criteria Set Up by Authorities in Municipal Finance.......... 74
    Findings in Cities in Which School and City Taxes Are Collected
      at the Same Time..................................... 75
    Conclusions.. 77
    Findings in Cities in Which School and City Taxes Are Collected
      Separately.. 77
  Summary.. 79

V. ADMINISTRATIVE CONTROL OF INCOME....................... 82
  Introduction.. 82
  Administrative Adjustments Preceding the Receipt of Tax Moneys. 82
    Need for Adjustments..................................... 82
    Adjustments Encountered.................................. 83
    Frequency of Occurrence of Adjustments.................... 83
    The Real Adjustment..................................... 85
  Administration of School Moneys............................. 86
    Custodian of School Moneys............................... 86
    Depositories... 86
    Current Surpluses.. 88
      Factors Creating Surpluses.............................. 88
    Returns from Current Surpluses............................ 89
      Interest Rates... 89
      Greater Returns from Deposits.......................... 89
      Larger Amounts on Deposit............................. 92
  Summary.. 97

CHAPTER   PAGE

VI. RECAPITULATIONS... 99
    The Tax Calendar and the Fiscal Year........................ 99
        Factors Delaying Tax Collection........................... 100
        Budgetary Review.. 100
        Submission of the Budget for Review....:.................. 101
        Cities in Which the Tax Calendar Has Been Coördinated with the
            Fiscal Year.. 102
        Collection of Taxes...................................... 103
        Fiscal Year Dates....................................... 104
    Internal Income Control.................................... 106
        Teachers' Retirement Fund................................ 106
        Capital Outlay and Debt Service........................... 106
    Administrative Control of Income............................ 107
        Custodian of School Funds................................ 107
        Interest on Balances..................................... 107
    Bibliography... 108

TABLES

NUMBER   PAGE

I. Cities and Villages Included in This Study Together with Their Population in 1925 and the Date Upon Which the School Fiscal Year Begins Therein.................................... 5

II. The Present Fiscal Status of the School Systems of New York Cities, Together with Their Fiscal Status, as Reported in Each of Nine Previous Studies Which Included Them............ 12

III. Summary Showing the Number of School Systems Operating Under Each Type of External Income Control in the Sixty Cities of New York State.............................. 15

IV. The Dates Here Given Show When the Annual School Estimate Was Approved by the Various Authorities in the Twenty-Two Cities Whose School Fiscal Year Began Jan. 1, 1926........ 17

V. The Dates Here Given Show When the Annual School Estimate Was Approved by the Various Authorities in the Twenty Cities and Six Villages Whose School Fiscal Year Began Aug. 1, 1925   18

VI. The Dates Here Given Show When the Annual School Estimate Was Approved by the Various Authorities in the City and Village Whose School Fiscal Years Began May 1, 1925, and July 1, 1925, Respectively............................. 19

VII. Individuals Responsible for the Preparation of the School Budget in Forty-Three Cities and Seven Villages in New York State... 25

VIII. Cities in Which Certain School Expenditures Are Omitted from the School Budget..................................... 27

IX. Procedure Being Followed by School Boards in Fourteen Cities and Two Villages in Budgeting for the State Teachers' Retirement Fund and State Moneys.......................... 33

X. Procedure Being Followed by School Boards in Six Cities in Budgeting for the State Teachers' Retirement Fund and State Moneys... 34

XI. Procedure Being Followed by the School Boards of Three Cities in Budgeting for the State Teachers' Retirement Fund and State Moneys... 35

XII. Procedure Being Followed by the School Boards in Sixteen Cities and Three Villages in Budgeting for the State Teachers' Retirement Fund and State Moneys.......................... 36

viii

NUMBER   PAGE

XIII. A Comparison Between Estimated and Actual Receipts, from Sources Other than Local Taxes, of the School Systems in Thirty-Four Cities and Six Villages During the Last Completed Fiscal Year   39

XIV. A Comparison Between Estimated and Actual Current Expense of the School Systems in Thirty-Seven Cities and Six Villages During the Last Completed Fiscal Year.................... 41

XV. Officials Who Levy and Collect School Taxes in Forty-Three Cities and Seven Villages in New York State............... 46

XVI. How Taxes Were Collected in 1917 and in 1927 in Forty-Three Cities and Seven Villages in New York State............... 48

XVII. Cities and Villages of this Study in Which School Taxes are Collected Separately or with Other Taxes.................. 50

XVIII. The Number of Days Which Elapsed Between the Beginning of the School Fiscal Year and the Date When Certain Events in the Tax Calendar of the Last Completed Fiscal Year Occurred 52

XIX. The Day Span Is Here Shown Between Certain Events in the School Tax Calendar of Twenty-Two Cities and One Village in Which School Taxes Were Collected as Early as Thirty-One Days After the Last Completed Fiscal Year Began.......... 58

XX. The Day Span Is Here Shown Between Certain Events in the School Tax Calendar of Twenty-One Cities and Six Villages in Which School Taxes Were Collected Later Than Thirty-One Days After the Beginning of the Last Completed School Fiscal Year.. 60

XXI. The Day Span Is Here Shown Between Certain Events in the School Tax Calendar of Seventeen Cities and Five Villages in Which School Taxes Are Collected Separate from All Other Taxes... 64

XXII. The Day Span Is Here Shown Between Certain Events in the School Tax Calendar in Eight Cities in Which School Taxes Are Collected at the Same Time as City Taxes................. 66

XXIII. The Day Span Is Here Shown Between Certain Events in the School Tax Calendar in Four Cities and Two Villages in Which School Taxes Are Collected with State and County Taxes.... 67

XXIV. The Day Span Is Here Shown Between Certain Events in the School Tax Calendar of Fourteen Cities in Which School Taxes Are Collected with State, County and City Taxes..... 69

XXV. The Day Span Is Here Shown Between Certain Events in the School Tax Calendar of Twenty Cities and Six Villages Whose School Fiscal Year Begins Aug. 1........................ 71

XXVI. The Day Span Is Here Shown Between Certain Events in the School Tax Calendar of Twenty-Three Cities Whose School Fiscal Year Begins Jan. 1.............................. 73

NUMBER   PAGE

XXVII. The Extent to Which School Funds Are Kept in Separate
Depositary Accounts in the Thirty-Five Cities in Which the
Custodian of City Funds Is also the Custodian of School Funds   87

XXVIII. Data on the Forty-Three Cities Studied Relative to Interest
Received on Depository Balances........................   90

XXIX. Balance in the School Funds in Village A at the End of Each
Month During the School Fiscal Years, Together with the
Parts of That Balance Which Were in the Two Depositories..   93

XXX. Balance in the School Fund in City B at the End of Each Month
During Two School Fiscal Years, Together with the Parts of
That Balance Which Were in the Two Depositories.........   94

XXXI. Balance in the School Fund in City C at the End of Each
Month During Three School Fiscal Years.................   95

XXXII. Balance in the School Fund in City D at the End of Each
Month During Three School Fiscal Years.................   95

XXXIII. Balance in the School Fund in City E at the End of Each
Month During Three School Fiscal Years.................   96

XXXIV. Balance in the School Fund in City F at the End of Each
Month During Three School Fiscal Years.................   96

CONTROL OF AVAILABLE PUBLIC SCHOOL INCOME

CHAPTER I

THE PROBLEM

Methods of Financial Control and Their Application to School Finance

There are many phases and methods of financial control in private, educational, municipal, state, and federal enterprises. Dr. F. A. Cleveland, former director of the Bureau of Municipal Research, New York City, a recognized authority on municipal finance, has designated five methods of effective financial control: (1) "Revenue control," (2) "Administrative discretionary control," (3) "Accounting control," (4) "Judicial control," and (5) "Popular control." He makes the following distinctions between these methods: [1]

1. Revenue control is secured through a representative house or council, in which all revenue measures must originate and whose action and approval are necessary to appropriation.

2. Administrative discretionary control is attained through the executive and through the various administrative discretionary heads subject to whose motion or discretion appropriations are disbursed.

3. Accounting control has more recently been added by the institution of a department or office, at the head of which is a comptroller, and in aid of which is devised a system of financial accounts.

4. Judicial control is found in an independently organized system of courts which may at all times be appealed to to enforce the performance of official duty and to protect municipal corporate rights.

5. Popular control—over council, executive, and financial officers—is secured through elections and appointments.

[1] Cleveland, F. A. *Chapters on Municipal Administration and Accounting*, pp. 62ff. Longmans, Green & Co. New York, 1909.

1

These methods of control are as applicable to public school finance as to the various financial aspects of purely municipal functions. In fact, there are many who contend that the operation of the schools is a municipal function and that the control of public school finance is but one phase of the control of municipal finance. This viewpoint, held largely by authorities in municipal government, is strongly opposed by leading authorities in educational administration.[2]

The controversy arising from these opposing viewpoints has centered around the method of "revenue control"; the main issue being whether the school board should be fiscally independent[3] or dependent[3] upon municipal authorities. Educators have supported their arguments with many objective studies.[4] Dr. Frasier[5] approached this problem from the historical, legal, and present school practice viewpoints. Present school practice was objectively and statistically evaluated by means of an index number. His conclusions are set forth in Chapter IX of his monograph.[6] Dr. McGaughy[7] applied a statistical technique to the various phases of school finance as well as to Frasier's "index of efficiency," that he might discover the existence of significant differences between the means of the obtainable measures from systems of both types of revenue control. His findings are summarized in Chapter V of his monograph.[8] In his recent book, Dr. Moehlman[9] devotes a chapter to this controversy, summarizing the schools of thought and critically examining the findings of the above studies.

The other methods of financial control designated by Dr. Cleveland have engaged the attention of educators as they have sought to apply scientific methods to the problems of school

[2] Strayer, G. D. and Engelhardt, N. L. *The Classroom Teacher*, pp. 28–29. American Book Company, 1920.

Cubberley, E. P. *Public School Administration.* pp. 104–5. Houghton Mifflin Company, 1922.

[3] For definition, see McGaughy, J. R. *The Fiscal Administration of City School Systems*, p. 2. The Macmillan Company, 1924.

[4] For the many studies to which reference will not be made herein see: Alexander, Carter. *Bibliography on Educational Finance.* The Macmillan Company, 1924.

[5] Frasier, Geo. W. *Control of City School Finances.* The Bruce Publishing Company, Milwaukee, Wis., 1922.

[6] *Ibid.*, pp. 83–87.

[7] *Op. cit.*, pp. 6ff.

[8] *Op. cit.*, pp. 55–56.

[9] Moehlman, Arthur B. *Public School Finance*, Chap. XIII, pp. 200–211. Rand McNally & Company, 1927.

finance. Dr. Smith [10] has studied the method of "administrative discretionary control" of public school finance in an effort to ascertain whether the "unit type" [11] or the "multiple type" [11] of administrative control is superior. Outstanding presentations concerning the method of "accounting control" as it pertains to school finance have been made by Hutchinson,[12] Fowlkes,[13] and Case.[14] "Judicial control" of school finances has had the attention of Henzlik,[15] Patty,[16] and Trusler.[17]

"Popular control" of school financial agents has been considered by Dr. Morrison [18] and Dr. McGaughy [19] in their studies relating to the superintendent and the board of education, respectively.

THE PRESENT STUDY

Statement of the Problem

The present study embraces an intensive investigation of certain phases of income control in the public school systems of the cities and larger villages of New York State. An attempt has been made to discover: (1) the types of revenue control which are operating within the state; (2) the effectiveness of present local budgetary control; (3) the extent to which public school moneys become available as needed; (4) the controls which are now affecting the timely receipt of public school income; (5) the adjustments which are made when school revenues are not received as

[10] Smith, H. P. *Business Administration of a City School System.* Bureau of Publications, Teachers College, Columbia University. New York, 1925.

[11] *Ibid.*, p. 4, for definition.

[12] Hutchinson, J. H. *School Costs and School Accounting.* Teachers College, Columbia University. Contributions to Education, No. 62, 1914.

[13] Fowlkes, J. G. *The Accounting of Public School Expenditures in Wisconsin.* Bureau of Educational Research, Bulletin No. 4, University of Wisconsin, 1924.

[14] Case, H. C. "Uniform Systems for Recording Disbursements for School Purposes as Prescribed for New York State." *American School Board Journal,* Vol. 53, pp. 24–26, 68, Oct., 1916.

[15] Henzlik, Frank E. *Rights and Liabilities of Public School Boards Under Capital Outlay Contracts.* Bureau of Publications, Teachers College, Columbia University, 1924.

[16] Patty, W. W. "Legal Provisions for Custody of and Liability for Public Funds for Secondary School Support." *American School Board Journal,* March, 1926, p. 47; April, 1926, p. 73.

[17] Trusler, Harry R. "Illegal Expenditures of School Money." *American School Board Journal,* Vol. 50, pp. 19–20, 78, Feb., 1915; pp. 18–19, 65, March, 1915.

[18] Morrison, J. Cayce. *The Legal Status of the City School Superintendent.* Warwick & York, Inc., 1922.

[19] *Op. cit.*, pp. 57ff.

needed; and (6) how moneys received in advance of need are being administered.

Scope of the Study

No attempt has been made to limit this study to any one of the methods of control designated by Cleveland.[20] Instead, it has been concerned with many of them as they are now operating in the school systems of the state. Nor has an effort been made to settle the controversy relative to the fiscal independence or dependence of school systems. Likewise, no attempt has been made to investigate possible sources of additional school income and the controls which should or should not be provided for its administration.

The well-informed person is aware of the fact that at present local taxation is the major source of school revenues. The percentage which moneys from this source bear to all school moneys varies from state to state and from locality to locality. In any locality where this percentage is large, much depends upon the machinery which has been set up to insure the availability of moneys from local taxation. The present study seeks to discover how this machinery is functioning in the cities and villages of New York State wherein moneys from local taxation constitute a large part of the funds available for the education of their children. While this is but one phase of the problem under investigation, as shown above, its solution has been considered of major importance by the writer, and has received fuller treatment than have the other phases enumerated above.

Sources of Data

The data used in this study are from two main sources: (1) school and municipal officials in forty-three cities and seven villages in New York State; (2) publications dealing with school and municipal finance. Minor sources include officials in state departments of education, students of educational administration, and legal publications.

Securing the Data

Fiscal Period for Which Data Were Secured. Unless otherwise stated, all field data used in this study pertain to the last completed school fiscal year of each system. With two exceptions,

[20] See p. 1.

these years ended July 31, or December 31, 1926. In those two systems the year in question ended April 30, and June 30, 1926.

TABLE I

CITIES AND VILLAGES INCLUDED IN THIS STUDY TOGETHER WITH THEIR POPULATION IN 1925, AND THE DATE UPON WHICH THE SCHOOL FISCAL YEAR BEGINS THEREIN

CITIES AND VILLAGES	POPULATION	DATE SCHOOL FISCAL YEAR BEGINS
CITIES		
Albany	117,820	Jan. 1
Amsterdam	35,260	Aug. 1
Auburn	35,677	Aug. 1
Batavia	15,628	Aug. 1
Beacon	11,621	Jan. 1
Canandaigua	7,686	Aug. 1
Cohoes	23,345	Jan. 1
Corning	15,722	Aug. 1
Dunkirk	19,912	Aug. 1
Elmira	48,359	Jan. 1
Fulton	12,571	Jan. 1
Geneva	15,908	Aug. 1
Glen Cove	10,822	Jan. 1
Glens Falls	17,851	Aug. 1
Gloversville	22,110	Aug. 1
Hornell	15,784	Aug. 1
Hudson	11,755	May 1
Jamestown	43,414	Aug. 1
Johnstown	10,712	Aug. 1
Lackawanna	20,196	Aug. 1
Little Falls	12,428	Jan. 1
Lockport	21,676	Jan. 1
Mechanicville	8,514	Aug. 1
Mount Vernon	50,382	Jan. 1
New Rochelle	44,222	Jan. 1
Niagara Falls	57,033	Aug. 1
North Tonawanda	17,356	Aug. 1
Norwich	8,345	Aug. 1
Olean	21,332	Aug. 1
Oneida	10,656	Jan. 1
Oneonta	12,057	Aug. 1
Oswego	22,369	Jan. 1
Poughkeepsie	35,670	Jan. 1
Rochester	316,786	Jan. 1
Rome	30,328	Jan. 1
Saratoga Springs	13,884	Jan. 1
Schenectady	92,786	Jan. 1
Syracuse	182,003	Jan. 1
Tonawanda	11,292	Aug. 1
Troy	72,223	Jan. 1
Utica	101,604	Jan. 1
Watervliet	16,158	Jan. 1
White Plains	27,428	Jan. 1

TABLE I *(Continued)*

CITIES AND VILLAGES	POPULATION	DATE SCHOOL FISCAL YEAR BEGINS
VILLAGES		
Green Island	4,510	Aug. 1
Hempstead	9,952	July 1
Herkimer	10,910	Aug. 1
Ilion	10,426	Aug. 1
Lynbrook	8,344	Aug. 1
Peekskill	17,993	Aug. 1
Seneca Falls	6,477	Aug. 1

School Systems Supplying the Data. Data were secured from forty-three cities and seven villages. These cities, shown in Table I, are entirely representative of the sixty cities of the state. It will be noted that the largest and smallest cities are not included in this study. All cities could not be included, and it was felt that the extremely large and small should be among those omitted. Any type of control known to exist in the state was found in at least one of the forty-five cities of this study. The seven villages, shown in Table I, are also believed to be representative of the villages of the state. These villages were included because of their size and the similarity of their problems to those of many of the cities studied. They are in different parts of the state, three being located in special legislation counties. Due to the uniformity of legislation affecting village school districts in the state, this number was considered sufficient for the purposes of this study.

The writer attempted to include data from cities and villages other than those in Table I, but due to local conditions sufficient data to warrant their inclusion were not procurable.

Method by Which Data Were Secured. A preliminary survey revealed that the necessary data with which to carry forward this study were not available in publications or state department files. It became evident that the individual school systems must be depended upon to supply the data sought. Investigatory visits to cities close to New York City showed that these data were in several places within the municipality often far removed from each other. It was, therefore, apparent that personal visitation to each city from which data were desired would be the only reliable method of securing the data sought.

Having reached this conclusion, it was obviously necessary to limit the territory to be covered. Two courses were open: (1) visit cities in several states within reach; or (2) confine the study to cities of one state. Even though involving greater travel costs, the latter course was chosen, and the study confined to cities and villages of New York State, although several cities in neighboring states were visited. This decision was influenced by the belief that a study of financial practices in the cities of one state would be of greater value to that state than a study involving cities of many states would be to any or all of them.

In order to insure the gathering of comparable data in each city visited, a checking list-questionnaire was prepared covering every phase of the controls to be studied. This was taken into each city and village and formed the basis for the conferences held by the writer in the fifty cities and villages shown in Table I. These conferences were held with both school and municipal officials. Due to the complexity of income control it was often necessary to consult from four to six local officials before all the data sought could be obtained. In some cases, due to inadequate records, it was impossible to secure all the facts desired. For this reason, some of the comparisons and analyses presented in the following chapters will involve fewer than forty-three cities and seven villages.

Other Data. Many of the data used in Chapter II were secured from studies which have been made of certain phases of revenue control. In subsequent chapters, other existing materials have been drawn upon from time to time. Data secured by means of correspondence have also been used.

Definition of Terms Used

Public School Income. There are two recognized kinds of public school income, revenue receipts and non-revenue receipts. Revenue receipts, or for simplicity of expression, revenues, may be defined as those moneys which come into the school treasury under such conditions that they increase assets without increasing liabilities. Non-revenue receipts, on the other hand, are moneys which come into the school treasury under such conditions that if they increase assets they also increase liabilities. Examples of revenues are: moneys from the federal government; from state, county, or local taxation; interest on cash balances, etc. Examples of non-revenue receipts are: moneys from sale of bonds; temporary loans; sale of buildings, etc. In this study, the term "receipts" is used for public school income whenever the source of the moneys received is not an issue. Whenever revenue receipts are meant, the term "revenues" is used.

Expenditure and Disbursement. The terms "expenditure" and "disbursement" will be used interchangeably in this study and will mean the actual outlay of moneys.

Expense. An expense and an expenditure are not synonymous and are not used interchangeably in this study. Much loose thinking in school finance has resulted from failure to differentiate clearly between these terms. The creation of an expense usually requires an expenditure, but an expenditure may not create an expense. An expense is a cost and may be incurred without an equivalent expenditure. For example, an expenditure for a school lunch room may or may not create an expense. If the money received from the sale of food is less than the expenditure made, the difference is an expense, but if the receipts are greater than the expenditures the difference is a revenue and no expense is involved.

The expense, however, may be greater than the expenditure made. For example, many states have a teachers' pension system to which the individual members thereof contribute. The school board very often deducts the amount of this contribution from one or more of the members' salary checks. In such cases the entire amount due the teacher is an expense to the school system and not merely the amount actually received by the teacher. The amount so deducted is not the property of the school district, for it only acts as the collecting agency for the state or local pension system and must turn over the amount so deducted in one way or another.

Income Control—External and Internal. For the purposes of this study, control of income is considered as being of two kinds, external and internal. This distinction is made on the basis of the type of control exercised over the income of a school system.

By external income control is meant the control which any reviewing authority outside the school system has over the amount to be raised for school during any period. This authority may or may not have absolute control over such amounts. By internal income control is meant the control which a board or its duly appointed representative exercises over the items and amounts which make up the total over which the external control operates.

The first of these controls, as it operates in the cities and villages of New York State, is considered in Chapter II. The second of these, internal or budgetary control, is the basis of the presentation in Chapter III.

Bibliography

On pages 108, 109 and 110 will be found a list of publications dealing with school and municipal finance. Whenever possible, these references are arranged alphabetically by authors. Only those publications to which specific reference has been made in this monograph are included in this bibliography. It, therefore, does not begin to include all the publications which were consulted during the investigation of this problem.

CHAPTER II

EXTERNAL INCOME CONTROL

INTRODUCTION

The controversy relative to the merits and demerits of the fiscally independent school system has not been settled on a state-wide basis in New York. While, as has been indicated, this study does not contemplate the solution of that problem, it seems advisable that the present stage reached in the process toward its ultimate solution on a state-wide basis be clearly set forth. A definite understanding of the present status of the school systems of the state relative to fiscal independence will doubtless contribute to an understanding of other phases of income control considered in the present study. Not only should the present status in this respect be known, but something of the changes preceding that status should be brought out.

PRESENT STATUS OF THE CITIES VISITED

In order to accomplish the objectives set forth in the preceding paragraph, all discoverable studies dealing with the fiscal dependence or independence of city school systems were examined for their findings relative to cities in New York State. In addition to these, the present status of the cities visited was made a part of this study. Table II shows a tabulation of the findings from these sources.

It is evident from a glance at Table II that all the cities of the state have not been included in each of these studies, so that the changes which may have occurred in the past quarter of a century may not all be shown thereby. Amsterdam, Rochester, and Utica have been included in all but two of these studies with no evidence of any change of status, except that Amsterdam is more independent now than in 1923. Several of the cities of the state have been reported upon by seven of the ten studies included in the tabulation of Table II.

Inasmuch as the present study did not include all the cities of the state, it must draw upon the last previous study to determine the present status of those not so included. In three cases, Hudson, Niagara Falls, and Elmira, there is a real disagreement between the findings of the present study and those reported by Dr. Gilbert[1] in 1924 for the same cities. Every study previous to the present one shows the school board in Hudson independent of municipal control. In actual practice, however, both school and city officials consider the school board dependent upon the board of estimate and apportionment for funds with which to run the schools. An examination of the statutes following the writer's conferences in that city failed to reveal any justification for this belief unless the $40 per capita, based on the total resident enrollment of the preceding year as guaranteed by the Law of 1921, Ch. 669, yields an insufficient fund for necessary school expenditures. On the basis of this evidence, Dr. Gilbert's report is accepted. Niagara Falls is clearly independent as provided by Law of 1922, Ch. 539 (in effect January 1, 1923). The school officials in that city have only during the past year come to realize the fact that their school board is not dependent upon the conception which municipal authorities have of school needs. This realization has encouraged them in their effort to secure credit for interest earned by school moneys on deposit. In the case of Elmira, no clue has been discovered which suggests the reason for the school board in that city being reported as fiscally independent by Dr. Gilbert.[2]

The minor disagreements in columns H and K as to independent versus special school districts in Dunkirk, Corning, Hornell, and Saratoga Springs are probably due to an assumption by Dr. Gilbert that inasmuch as the limits of these school districts are not coterminous with the cities' limits, the budget is presented to the legal voters for adoption. In the first three of these cities, the writer was assured by a responsible local school official that the budget was not passed upon by others than the school board. In Saratoga Springs, however, the budget is presented to the common council for the approval which it cannot withhold.

---

[1] Gilbert, Frank B. "Some Legal Aspects of the City School Problem." Reprint, *Journal of New York State Teachers Association*, Jan., 1924.

[2] *Ibid.*, p. 5.

TABLE II

The Present Fiscal Status of the School Systems of New York Cities, Together with Their Fiscal Status, as Reported in Each of Nine Previous Studies Which Included Them

Cities	+A 1902	+B 1917	+C 1920	+E 1921	+F 1921	+G 1922	+H 1923	+J 1924	+K 1924	+L 1927	+P 1927
1 Albany		I	D	I**	I**		D**	I	D	D	D
2 Amsterdam			I	I	I		I**		I	I	I*
3 Auburn			I				I*		I	I	S
4 Batavia		D	I	I	I				S	S	I*
5 Beacon	D		D				D	D	D	I	D
6 Binghamton	I		D				D		D		D
7 Buffalo			I	I	I	D			S	S	S
8 Canandaigua			I				I*		I	I	I*
9 Cohoes			I	I**	I**		I**	I	S	I	I**
10 Corning			D				I**	D	I		D
11 Cortland			I				I**	I	S	I	I**
12 Dunkirk			I	I**	I**			I	I	I**	S
13 Elmira			D				D**		S	S	I**
14 Fulton			I	I**	I**		I**	I	I	I**	I*
15 Geneva			I				I**		S	S	I*
16 Glen Cove			I					I	I		I*
17 Glens Falls			I		I**		I**		S	I**	I*
18 Gloversville			I						I	I	I**
19 Hornell				I	I				S	D	I**
20 Hudson			I						I		S
21 Ithaca			I					I	I	I	I*
22 Jamestown		I	I	I**	I**		I**		I	I**	I*
23 Johnstown		I	I		I**		I**		I		I**
24 Kingston			I	I					I		I**
25 Lackawanna			I		I				S	S	S
26 Little Falls			I						I	I	I*
27 Lockport			I						I	I	I*
28 Long Beach									I	I	S
29 Mechanicville			I						I	S	I*
30 Middletown			I						S		I**
31 Mount Vernon			D	I**	I**		I**	I	I	I**	I**
32 Newburgh		D	D	I*	I*				I		I**
33 New Rochelle		D	D	I**		D	I**	D	I	I**	I**
34 New York	D	D	I						D		D
35 Niagara Falls			I				D*		D	I	I*
36 North Tonawanda			I				I*		S	S	S
37 Norwich							I*		S	S	S
38 Ogdensburg				I	I				S		I*

#	City	A	B	C	E	F	G	H	J	K	L	P
39	Olean			I						S	S	S
40	Oneida			I	I**	I**		I**	I	I	I	I*
41	Oneonta			I	I**	I**		I**		I	I**	I**
42	Oswego			D				I**		I	I	I**
43	Plattsburg			I				I*		I		S
44	Port Jervis			I		I*				I	D	D
45	Poughkeepsie		D	D	I**	I*		I**	D	S		I**
46	Rensselaer	D	D	I				D	D	D	D	D
47	Rochester	D		I	I**	I**	D	D		I	I**	I**
48	Rome	D		I	I**	I**		I**		I	I**	I**
49	Salamanca			I	I	I		I*		I		I*
50	Saratoga Springs			D				D	I	S	I	D
51	Schenectady			I				D	D	D	D	I*
52	Sherrill		D	D				D				D
53	Syracuse	D		I	I	I		I*		D	D	I*
54	Tonawanda		D	I				D		I	I	D
55	Troy	D		D				I*		D	I	I*
56	Utica		D	I	I**	I**		I**		I	I	I**
57	Watertown			I	I**	I**		I**		I		I**
58	Watervliet			I	I**	I**		I**			I**	I**
59	White Plains	D		I						I	I**	I**
60	Yonkers		D	D				D		D		D
	Number of Cities	8	14	59	27	27	3	48	18	57	44	60

+ Explanation of letters used in Table II.

I   Fiscally independent. See footnote 3, p. 2.

D   Fiscally dependent. See footnote 3, p. 2.

S   Budget voted on by legal voters.

I*   School budget either not submitted for review or reviewer has no authority to change it.

I**   School board submits budget to municipal officials who may reduce it, but the school board can replace original amount by a three-fourths vote.

Studies reporting the fiscal status of New York State school system.

A—Rollins, Frank. *School Administration in Municipal Government*, pp. 24ff. Columbia University Contributions to Philosophy, Vol. II, 1902.

B—Deffenbaugh, W. S. *Current Practice in City School Administration*, pp. 32ff. U. S. Bulletin, No. 8, 1917.

C—*Report of Special Joint Committee on Taxation and Retrenchment*, pp. 30–31. New York State Legislature, Legislative Document, No. 80. Lyons Co., Albany, 1920.

E—Gilbert, Frank M. *Extract from Memorandum on Senate Bill*, Printed Number 425, February 23, 1921.

F—Allen, R. F. *Unpublished Study*, December, 1921. (On file in Legal Division of State Department of Education, Albany).

G—Frasier, Geo. W. *Control of City School Finances.* The Bruce Publishing Company, Milwaukee, Wis. 1922.

H—Strayer, G. D., and Haig, R. M. *The Financing of Education in the State of New York*, p. 177. The Macmillan Company. 1923.

J—McGaughy, J. R. *Fiscal Administration of City School Systems.* The Macmillan Company, 1924.

K—Gilbert, Frank M. "Some Legal Aspects of the City School Problem." Reprint, *Journal of the New York State Teachers' Association*, January, 1924.

L—From data gathered by the writer, 1927.

P—Present status as shown by the findings of the present study or of the last previous study including cities in New York State.

Because of the virtual agreement between the findings of these last two studies when they involve the same cities, the report of Dr. Gilbert[3] is accepted as the present status of any city system not included in the present study. For any city not included in either of these last two studies the status last reported is assumed to be the present status of that system. This assumption must be made for only two cities, viz. Ogdensburg and Sherrill. In column P, opposite each city, will be found a code letter which will reveal the present status of that city's school system relative to fiscal independence.

Trend Toward Fiscal Independence of School Boards

An analysis of Table II shows that during the past twenty-five years, in only one city, Buffalo, has the school system changed from a fiscally independent to a fiscally dependent one. In contrast to this, the school system in six cities—Beacon, Newburgh, New Rochelle, Niagara Falls, Oswego and Watertown—has changed from fiscal dependence to fiscal independence. The trend toward fiscal independence is an unmistakable one. In the judgment of leading authorities in educational administration this trend is highly desirable.

This finding is also in harmony with the findings of Dr. Morehart[4] in a recent study covering the United States. In an unpublished digest of his findings he says:

There is an increasing tendency to grant to boards of education as agents of the state, the sole power to levy school taxes and to expend the income thereof, and to secure the right to levy exceptionally high taxes by submitting the question to a vote of the people.

Column P of Table II shows that in eleven, or over 18 per cent of the cities of the state, the school system is fiscally dependent. Nine of these eleven are included in the ten largest cities of the state according to 1925 population figures, with Utica, which ranks seventh in population, the only city among the first ten having a fiscally independent school system. In twenty-three, or over 38 per cent, of the cities, the school board either does not have to present its budget to reviewing authorities or else those to whom it is presented have no choice but to accept it. In sixteen, or nearly 27 per cent, of the cities, the budget must be

[3] *Ibid.*, pp. 5, 6.

[4] Morehart, G. C.   *The Legal Status of City School Boards.*   Bureau of Publications, Teachers College, Columbia University, 1927.

presented to the municipal officials for review and adoption, but if those officials see fit to reduce the amounts carried by the budget, the school board can readopt the original budget if three-fourths of the board members so vote. In ten, or nearly 17 per cent, of the cities, the school budget must be voted upon favorably by the legal voters at an annual school meeting before it becomes an operative document.

Table III summarizes the analysis presented in the above paragraph.

TABLE III

Summary Showing the Number of School Systems Operating under Each Type of External Income Control in the Sixty Cities of New York State

Types of School Systems	No. of School Systems of Each Type	Percentage of Total Systems Having Each Type
a Dependent	11	18.33
b Absolutely Independent	23	38.33
c Virtually Independent	16	26.67
d Special	10	16.67
Total	60	100.00

a See note D Table II.
b See note I* Table II.
c See note I** Table II.
d See note S Table II.

BUDGETARY REVIEW

Personnel

It should be of interest to discover who reviews the school budget in the fifty cities and villages included in this study. In all villages of the state and in nine of the forty-three cities studied the school budget is reviewed by the legal voters. This is doubtless a hangover from the town meeting days and is now little short of a rubber stamp approval. In nine of the cities, it is first reviewed by the board of estimate and apportionment and then by the common council. In fourteen of the cities it is presented directly to the common council for review, and in four cities the budget after adoption by the board of education need not be presented for further review. In the remaining seven cities the budget is presented to the mayor for review, and in three of these seven it is adopted by the common council after being approved by the mayor. In three of these seven cities the mayor meets with the school board when it is considering the school budget. Thus it is evident that, although more than three-fourths of the school boards of the state are actually or virtually fiscally independent,[5] in most of these cities the annual estimate must be approved by municipal authorities before the net amount provided in it can be raised by local taxation. The time consumed in this legislative checking process will be brought out later in this chapter.

Adoption of the Budget by the School Board and Its Submission for Review

A comparison of the date when the school board adopted the annual estimate with the date when this estimate is legally required to be submitted to the proper reviewing authority in the cities of this study is illuminating. Table IV contains those cities in which the school fiscal year for which dates were secured began January 1, 1926. Table V contains those cities and villages in which dates for the budget calendar were secured for the school fiscal year beginning August 1, 1925. The city of Hudson and the village of Hempstead, in Table VI, were the only school systems visited whose fiscal year did not begin either January 1 or August 1. No valid reason could be discovered for these systems having fiscal years beginning May 1 and July 1, respectively.

Analysis of Tables IV, V, and VI. Proceeding from left to right in these tables the following dates will be found after each city: the date when the school budget or annual estimate is required to be presented to the first reviewing authority in that city; the date when this annual estimate was adopted by the board of education therein; and the date when the various reviewing authorities accepted this or an adjusted estimate.

A study of column 3 in these tables shows that in eleven of the thirty-nine cities pertinent to this analysis, the estimate involved was adopted by the school board from fourteen to one hundred and six days after the date required for submission to the reviewing authority. Four of these school boards had delayed such approval for more than two months after the required date. At best, this is not a creditable showing. A larger percentage of the cities in

[5] See footnote, Table III, p. 75.

TABLE IV

The Dates Here Given Show When the Annual School Estimate Was Approved by the Various Authorities in the Twenty-Two Cities Whose School Fiscal Year Began Jan. 1, 1926.

CITIES	1 — DATE ANNUAL ESTIMATE IS TO BE SUBMITTED FOR REVIEW (a)	2 — DATE ANNUAL ESTIMATE WAS APPROVED BY SCHOOL BOARD	3 — DAYS FROM DATE IN COLUMN 1 TO DATE IN COLUMN 2 (b)	4 — DATE ANNUAL ESTIMATE WAS APPROVED BY MAYOR OR BOARD OF ESTIMATE (c)	5 — DATE ANNUAL ESTIMATE WAS APPROVED BY ELECTORATE OR COMMON COUNCIL (d)	6 — DAYS FROM DATE IN COLUMN 2 TO DATE IN COLUMN 4 (b)	7 — DAYS FROM DATE IN COLUMN 2 TO DATE IN COLUMN 5	8 — DAYS FROM DATE IN COLUMN 4 TO DATE IN COLUMN 5 (b)
Albany	Nov. 1	Oct. 20, '25	−12	B Nov. 12, '25	C Dec. 7, '25	23	48	25
Beacon	Oct. 1	Sept. 22, '25	−9	B Feb. 5, '26	C Dec. 20, '25	46	89	12
Cohoes	Dec. 1	Dec. 21, '25	20		C Feb. 17, '26		58	
Elmira	Oct. 1	Sept. 28, '25	−3		C Nov. 4, '25		37	
Fulton	Oct. 1–15	Oct. 29, '25	14	M Sept. 15, '25	C Oct. 18, '25	−22	50	28
Glen Cove	Sept. 1	Oct. 7, '25	36		C Oct. 13, '25		6	
Little Falls	Mar. 15	Mar. 9, '26	−6		C Apr. 15, '26		37	
Lockport	June 1	May 29, '25	−3	B June 29, '25	C July 13, '25	31	45	14
Mount Vernon	Oct. 1	Oct. 27, '25	26	M Oct. 30, '25	C Nov. 24, '25	3	28	25
New Rochelle	Jan. 25	Jan. 20, '26	−5	B Mar. 12, '26	C Mar. 16, '26	51	55	4
Oneida	Oct. 1–10	Oct. 7, '25	−3	M Oct. 7, '25		0	0(e)	
Oswego	May 1	Apr. 20, '26	−11		C July 1, '26		72	
Poughkeepsie	Oct. 1	Sept. 24, '25	−7		C Oct. 31, '25		37	
Rochester	Dec. 31	Dec. 30, '25	−1	B Feb. 13, '26	C Mar. 9, '26	45	69	24
Rome	Sept. 1	Oct. 5, '25	34		C Oct. 19, '25		14	
Saratoga Springs	Oct. 1	Sept. 25, '25	−6		C Oct. 30, '25		35	
Schenectady	Nov. 1	Oct. 15, '25	−17	B Oct. 31, '25	C Nov. 4, '25	16	20	4
Syracuse	Nov. 1	Feb. 15, '26	106	B Mar. 8, '26	C Mar. 15, '26	21	28	7
Troy	Nov. 1	Oct. 15, '25	−16	B Dec. 18, '25	C Dec. 17, '25	64	63	−1
Utica	Nov. 1	Oct. 30, '25	−2	B Feb. 27, '26	C Mar. 17, '26	120	138	18
Watervliet	Nov. 1	Dec. 9, '25	38		C Dec. 18, '25		9	
White Plains	Aug. 15	July 24, '25	−22	M July 24, '25	C Oct. 20, '25	0	88	88
Number of Cases			22			13	22	12
Range			−22 to 106			−22 to 120	0 to 138	−1 to 88
Median			−3.7			23	41	16

(a) These dates were checked with those given in Allen's study—see note F, Table II.

(b) A minus sign preceding a number indicates that the date mentioned second in the columnar heading preceded the date mentioned first in that heading.

(c) "B" preceding date indicates approval by the board of estimate. "M" preceding date indicates approval by the mayor.

(d) "C" preceding date indicates approval by the common council. "E" preceding date indicates approval by the legal voters.

(e) Repeated from column 6 because the Mayor was the final reviewing authority

How to Read Tables IV, V, and VI: In Albany the annual school estimate for the last completed fiscal year was adopted by the school board on Oct. 20, 1925, 12 days before it was required to be submitted for review, i.e., Nov. 1. It was approved by the board of estimate on Nov. 12, 1925, and by the common council on Dec. 7, 1925, 23 and 48 days, respectively, after the adoption by the school board. Twenty-five days elapsed between the date of approval by the board of estimate and by the common council.

TABLE V

The Dates Here Given Show When the Annual School Estimate Was Approved by the Various Authorities in the Twenty Cities and Six Villages Whose School Fiscal Year Began Aug. 1, 1925

Cities and Villages	1 — Date Annual Estimate Is to Be Submitted for Review (a)	2 — Date Annual Estimate Was Approved by School Board	3 — Days from Date in Column 1 to Date in Column 2 (b)	4 — Date Annual Estimate Was Approved by Mayor or Board of Estimate (c)	5 — Date Annual Estimate Was Approved by Electorate or Common Council (b)	6 — Days from Date in Column 2 to Date in Column 4	7 — Days from Date in Column 2 to Date in Column 5	8 — Days from Date in Column 4 to Date in Column 5
Cities								
Amsterdam	Jan. 15	Mar. 25, '25	69		C Apr. 7, '25		13	
Auburn	May 15	May 11, '25	-4		C May 19, '25		8	
Batavia	1st Tues. in August (f)	July 25, '25	-10		E Aug. 4, '25		10	
Canandaigua	1st Tues. in May (e)	Apr. 17, '25	-18		E May 5, '25		18	
Corning		Aug. 31, '25						
Dunkirk		Aug. 10, '25						
Geneva	1st Tues. May	May 1, '25	-4		E May 5, '25		4	
Glens Falls	1st Tues. May	Apr. 3, '25	-32		E May 5, '25		32	
Gloversville	Mar. 1	Feb. 20, '25	-9	M Mar. 1, '25		9	9(e)	
Hornell		Aug. 17, '25						
Jamestown		May 4, '25						
Johnstown	July 1	June 25, '25	-6		E Aug. 4, '25	6	6(e)	
Lackawanna	1st Tues. May	July 28, '25	84		E Aug. 4, '25		6	
Mechanicville	1st Tues. Aug.	July 24, '25	-11		E Mar. 18, '25		11	
Niagara Falls	Apr. 1	Feb. 27, '25	-33	M July 1, '25	C Mar. 4, '25		19	
North Tonawanda	1st Tues. Aug.	July 8, '25	-27		E Aug. 5, '25		27	
Norwich	1st Tues. May	May 4, '25	-1		E May 5, '25		1	
Olean	1st Tues. May	Apr. 23, '25	-12		E May 5, '25		12	
Oneonta	July 15	July 7, '25	-8	M July 15, '25	C May 4, '25	8	8(e)	
Tonawanda	Feb. 1	Apr. 6, '25	64				28	
Villages								
Green Island	1st Tues. May	May 1, '25	-4		E May 5, '25		4	
Herkimer	2d Tues. Aug.	July 1, '25	-41		E Aug. 11, '25		41	
Ilion	1st Tues. Aug.	June 1, '25	-64		E Aug. 4, '25		64	
Lynbrook	1st Tues. May	Apr. 3, '25	-32		E May 5, '25		32	
Peekskill	1st Tues. May	Apr. 28, '25	-7		E May 5, '25		7	
Seneca Falls	1st Tues. May	Apr. 29, '25	-6		E May 12, '25		13	
Number of cases			22			3	22	
Range			-64 to 84			6 to 9	1 to 64	
Median			-8.5			8	11.5	

(a), (b), (c), (d), (e). Same as Table IV.   (e) 1st Tues. in May was May 5, 1925.
(f) 1st Tues. in August was Aug. 4, 1925.   *How to Read Table V*: See Explanation following Table IV. p. 17.

TABLE VI+

The Dates Here Given Show When the Annual School Estimate Was Approved by the Various Authorities in the City and Village Whose School Fiscal Years Began May 1, 1925 and July 1, 1925, Respectively. A Summary of Measures for All Cities in Tables IV, V, and VI Is Also Given

Cities and Villages	1 Date Annual Estimate Is To Be Submitted For Review (a)	2 Date Annual Estimate Was Approved By Board	3 Days from the Date in Column 1 to Date in Column 2 (b)	4 Date Annual Estimate Was Approved by Mayor or Board of Estimate (c)	5 Date Annual Estimate Was Approved by Electorate or Common Council (d)	6 Days from Date in Column 2 to Date in Column 4	7 Days from Date in Column 2 to Date in Column 5	8 Days from Date in Column 4 to Date in Column 5
City Fiscal year—May 1 to April 30 Hudson	Sept. 10	Oct. 13, '24	33		C Nov. 20, '24		38	
Village Fiscal year—July 1 to June 30 Hempstead	1st Tues. May	Apr. 15, '25	−20		E May 5, '25		20	

+ Explanations of a b c d for this table are the same as those for Tables IV and V.

SUMMARY OF MEASURES FIGURED FOR ALL CITIES AND VILLAGES IN TABLES IV, V, AND VI

	3	6	7	8
Number of Cases	46	16	46	12
Range	−64 to 106	−22 to 120	0 to 138	−1 to 88
Median	−6	18.5	27.5	16

Table IV than those in Table V, were offenders in this matter but the three in the latter group were all among the worst offenders. As a group, the cities whose school fiscal year began January 1 do not measure up to the cities and villages whose school fiscal year begins August 1. The median city in the former group adopted its estimate 3.7 days before the date set for its submission for review, while the median city in the latter group adopted its estimate 8.5 days before that date. When all of the thirty-nine cities and seven villages were considered as a group, it was found that the median city adopted its estimate 6 days before the date set for its submission for review.[6]

Assuming that the various dates set for the submission of the annual estimates for review have been wisely chosen, there seems to be no valid reason why these estimates should have been adopted by the school boards all the way from sixty-four days before to one hundred and six days after the date set for such submission. Obligation to legal provisions should be strong enough to prevent undue delay in adopting the annual estimate, and sound budgetary procedure does not provide for the adoption of the annual estimate far in advance of requirements. If the date for the submission of the annual estimate for review is not properly chosen in light of all the events which make up the tax calendar, then it should be changed, and the adoption of the annual estimate by the board properly coördinated therewith. In a subsequent chapter, the factors involved in a wise choice of the dates which make up the tax calendar will be set forth and a constructive program squaring with sound business practice and the findings of this study will be presented.

Time Consumed in Review

It has been shown that in all but four cities included in this study the annual estimate is submitted for review after being adopted by the board of education. How soon thereafter was the budget approved in its final form? Columns 6, 7, and 8 of Tables IV, V, and VI contain this information. In column 7 will be found the number of days which elapsed from the date on which the annual estimate was adopted by the school board until its final approval by the reviewing authority. This column reveals the fact that from no days, in the case of Oneida, to one hundred and thirty-eight days, in the case of Utica, were consumed in this

[6]See Table VI, p. 19.

review. It is also evident that the number of days required for this action is not a function of the type of external income control in operation nor is it a function of the size of the city.

A comparison of this time span in the cities included in Tables IV and V, respectively, shows that a much greater time was consumed in this process in the cities whose school fiscal year begins January 1, than in the cities whose school fiscal year begins August 1. In the median city of the former group, forty-one days were taken up with review, while in the median city of the latter group only 11.5 days were required. In the median city of the entire group of thirty-nine cities and seven villages, disregarding fiscal year dates, 27.5 days lapsed before the budget was finally approved. The greater lapse of time in performing this function in cities whose school fiscal year begins January 1 was doubtless due to the multitudinous duties which confronted the municipal officials at the time when the school budget was submitted for review. In all but four of these cities,[7] the school tax is collected at the same time as the general city tax. This means that all the other departmental estimates are being considered at the same time as the school estimate. The adoption of the school budget, although satisfactory as to amount, is often delayed because of its being considered an integral part of the general city budget. In only three of the cities in Table V is the school budget in this way dependent upon the general city budget.

It is interesting to note that in the twelve cities of Table IV where there are two reviewing authorities in addition to the school board this fact does not necessarily cause the total elapsed time to be large. In eight of the nine cities, however, in which the board of estimate was the first of these two reviewing authorities, the greater portion of the total time consumed in the review was taken by that authority. This indicates that the common council, or second reviewing authority, accepts the judgment of the board of estimate without much investigation. In view of this fact, the wisdom of requiring this second review of the school budget seems questionable. In all of these cities but Lockport, however, the school tax is collected with the general city tax[8] so that the school budget must wait on the general city budget for adoption. Thus, it is evident that under present conditions but slight gain would

[7] See Table XVII, Chap. IV, p. 50.

[8] See Table XVII. Chap. IV, p. 50.

result to the schools if this second reviewing authority were abolished.

The whole problem of when the annual estimate should be submitted for review, the maximum length of time to be consumed in that review, and the effect which these factors have and should have upon the availability of school moneys when needed will be treated in a subsequent chapter.

SUMMARY

The first part of this chapter showed the present status of the city school systems of New York State relative to their dependence upon city authorities for moneys with which to provide adequate educational programs. Previous studies involving many of these cities furnish a study of the changes which have taken place in this regard. In only one city has the school system become dependent after having been independent, while six systems have become independent since one or more of these studies were made. At present eleven cities of the state are fiscally dependent, thirty-nine are either absolutely or virtually fiscally independent,[9] and ten, while not fiscally dependent upon city officials, must have their budgets approved by the voters at an annual school meeting.

Budgetary review procedure in forty-three cities of the state was shown in the remainder of this chapter. In only four city systems studied was it unnecessary for the school board to submit its budget for review. In twenty-six of the other thirty-nine cities, the budget was approved by the common council. In twelve of these twenty-six, it had been previously approved by either the mayor or the board of estimate.

Eleven school boards in these cities did not adopt their budget until after the date legally required for its submission to the reviewing authority. Four of these boards were more than two months late. The group of cities whose school fiscal year begins August 1 came nearer to conforming to the required date for submission than the group whose school year begins January 1. The reviewing authorities in the latter group also took a much longer time to review the school budget than was the case in the former group.

It was found that the number of days which elapsed from the date when the budget was adopted by the school board until the

⁹ See footnote, Table III, p. 15.

date when finally approved by the reviewing authority was not dependent upon either the type of external income control exercised or the size of the city.

It was also shown that when two authorities review the budget after its adoption by the school board some time could be saved by omitting the second authority which usually takes a very much shorter time to review the school budget than the first. In only one case, however, would this be beneficial to the schools under present conditions, for in all the other cities the school tax is collected at the same time as the general city tax.

CHAPTER III

INTERNAL INCOME CONTROL

INTRODUCTION

As stated in the preceding chapter, some of the practices relating to internal control of school finances in the various cities of the state will be presented in this chapter. No attempt will be made to present an exhaustive treatise on budgetary procedure. Many such presentations are now available, awaiting the attention of the reader. In addition to standard treatises on the budget there are many publications dealing specifically with the school budget which deserve the attention of school men in the field. Among the most recent of these presentations are articles and books by Engelhardt and Engelhardt,[1] Daley,[2] Pittenger,[3] and Moehlman.[4]

The aim of this part of the study was to discover present practice in certain phases of budgetary control, and to apply accepted principles of sound budgetary procedure to the solution of the problems so discovered to the end that present practice might be benefited thereby. Data with which to answer questions such as the following were secured. Who is responsible for the preparation of the budget? What expenditure and income items are not carried in the budget? How accurate have the estimates for income and expenditure proved to be? To what extent is an allowance being made in the budget for retirement fund payments during the fiscal period covered by the budget? To a consideration of these phases of budgetary control and the findings relative thereto, this chapter will be devoted.

[1] Engelhardt, N. L., and Engelhardt, Fred. "Budgetary Practices in Local School Systems." *Teachers College Record*, Dec., 1926, pp. 394–412.

[2] Daley, R. L. "School Accounting Officers and Relations to the Preparation of the Budget." *Fourteenth Annual Proceedings, National Association of Public School Business Officials*, 1925, p. 66.

[3] Pittenger, B. F. *An Introduction to Public School Finance*, pp. 45–72. Houghton Mifflin Company, 1925.

[4] Moehlman, A. E. *Public School Finance*, Chap. XI, pp. 172–186; Part III, pp. 229–281 Rand, McNally & Company, 1927.

THE BUDGET

Every superintendent or school official interviewed assured the writer that his school system was being operated in accordance with a well-formulated annual school budget. When their budgets for the last completed fiscal year were examined, it was evident that a "well-formulated budget" meant different things to each of them. In a few systems, no budget was on file, an entry in the minutes of the board showing the amount of the net budget being the only record available. Many of the school men of the state, however, are in step with scientific movements in education and are developing their budgets in accordance with accepted budgetary principles.

TABLE VII

INDIVIDUALS RESPONSIBLE FOR THE PREPARATION OF THE SCHOOL BUDGET IN FORTY-THREE CITIES AND SEVEN VILLAGES IN NEW YORK STATE

	NUMBER OF CITIES IN WHICH COMBINATION WAS FOUND
Superintendent	
1. Alone	6
2. With business manager or clerk of the board	15
3. With finance committee	10
4. With board	5
5. With clerk and finance committee	2
6. With clerk and board	1
	— 39
Business Manager or Clerk of the Board	
7. Alone	4
8. With board	1
	— 5
Finance Committee	
9. Alone	1
10. With president of the board	1
11. With clerk	1
Board	
12. Alone	2
Member of Board	
13. Alone	1
	— 50

PREPARATION OF THE BUDGET

Table VII presents in detail the various officials involved in the major activities of budget preparation. It shows that in thirty-nine of the fifty New York cities and villages visited the superintendent has a part in making up the tentative budget. However, the degree of activity being exercised by that executive officer varies greatly within the state. Merely a cursory glance at the table reveals the variation which was found in the preparation of this important document.

In only twenty-one cities could it be said that the budget is being prepared in accordance with universally accepted principles of budgetary procedure. In these twenty-one cities either the superintendent prepares the budget or it is prepared under his direction by the business manager or clerk of the board. The part which committee action of the board is allowed to play in the formulation of the budget is contrary to the recommendations of authorities on budgetary procedure. It seems almost incredible that in eleven instances out of fifty the superintendent of schools has no major part in the formulation of the budget in a state which has had the educational leadership with which this state has been blessed. More and more the executive budget is replacing the legislative budget in municipal and school finance. This is due to the growing realization that it is the executive and his assistants who are informed relative to the needs and costs which largely govern the amounts to be provided in the budget. The function of the school board in budgetary procedure is to make sure that that document is adequate to carry forward the plans which have been formulated and approved. Engelhardt and Engelhardt[5] have well expressed this principle of budgetary responsibility:

A consistent application of sound administration principles will place on the superintendent of schools the responsibilities for the preparation, the validation, and the operation of the budget. The school board, however, should approve the budget as it does other policies or administrative acts. . . . Since the administration of the budget is associated with the current operations of the school system, budgetary responsibilities may be delegated, and the business office may be directly responsible for its preparation as in the case of all financial statements and reports.

ITEMS NOT INCLUDED IN THE BUDGET

Experience has shown that when a school system is considered as a department of the city government, many school services are often paid for out of general city funds and therefore are not

[5] See footnote [1], p. 24.

included in the school budget. In such cases the city officials usually retain control of the purse strings. The school expenditures which are most often omitted from the school budget under such conditions are those for "capital outlay" and "debt service." Table VIII shows the situation in the cities visited relative to such omissions from the school budget.

TABLE VIII

CITIES IN WHICH CERTAIN SCHOOL EXPENDITURES ARE
OMITTED FROM THE SCHOOL BUDGET

THOSE OMITTING CAPITAL OUTLAY (ONLY)	THOSE OMITTING DEBT SERVICE (ONLY)	THOSE OMITTING BOTH CAPITAL OUTLAY AND DEBT SERVICE
Cities White Plains	Cities Fulton * Glens Falls Hudson Oswego Syracuse Watervliet	Cities Albany Glen Cove New Rochelle Poughkeepsie Schenectady Troy Utica
	Villages Green Island	

* City officials add charges for debt service to school tax rate.

Capital Outlay and Debt Service

In eight[6] of the forty-three cities included in this analysis no item appears in the school budget for capital outlay, and in thirteen cities and one village no item appears for debt service. However, in one of these latter cities, Fulton, the amount for debt service is included in the school tax rate by the municipal authorities. In seven of these cities the school board includes no amount for either capital outlay or debt service; in one, capital outlay only is omitted; and in six cities and one village debt service only is excluded. Of the seven which omit both capital outlay and debt service from their budgets, four are fiscally dependent, one is fiscally independent, and two have power to replace any amount reduced by the reviewing authority[7]. In the city omitting capital outlay only from its budget, the school board has final

[6] See Table VIII, for the cities discussed in this paragraph.
[7] See Table II p. 12.

authority over the amount to be spent for other school services[8]. Concerning the six cities whose school boards do not include expenses for debt service in their budget, only one is fiscally dependent; one has its budget approved at the annual school meeting; two are fiscally independent; and two are virtually independent[9]. Thus it is evident that there is no direct relationship between the dependence of the school system and divided authority in budgeting for complete school expenditures.

It is evident that in these cities school authorities are not responsible for the preparation of a complete budget. Since each group of authorities has a part in determining the amounts which shall make up the total school budget, no one set of officials is responsible for the gross amount to be spent on the schools in any fiscal year. This procedure often leaves the citizens uninformed concerning the total cost of education to the local community. It is an accepted principle of school administration that the school authorities should have complete authority over the entire budget. This establishes direct responsibility for all school expenditures and is far superior to the divided responsibility found in many cities of the state. To discontinue this divided authority would be a distinct step forward in the march toward sound administrative practices.

Another omission from the budget and its effect on budgetary control deserves special treatment. The next section will be devoted to its consideration.

Teachers' Retirement Fund

Present Method of Maintenance. In the study which was made of the items which are being included in the budget, the procedures relative to the inclusion of amounts for the teachers' retirement fund of the state were found to be anything but uniform and in accordance with sound budgetary practices. Chapter 503 of the Law of 1920, effective August 1, 1921, provided for a "State Teachers' Retirement Fund for Public School Teachers." This fund is administered by a retirement board in the State Department of Education. The fund is maintained through contributions amounting to 4 per cent of each member's annual salary, to be paid by the member, and 5.2 per cent of the annual salary of each public school teacher in the state to be paid by the several district

[8] *Ibid.*
[9] *Ibid.*

school boards, according to the salaries of all teachers within their respective districts, out of funds regularly provided for meeting school needs.

The present method of paying this money into the retirement fund has occasioned considerable misunderstanding in local school systems, and has provided an opportunity for the exercise of unsound budgetary practices. Each year the several school districts of the state receive moneys from the state, the largest payments usually being received in April and May. Under the system now in operation, the Administration Division of the State Department of Education, through which state moneys are apportioned to the several school districts, deducts from state moneys due a given district the retirement fund contribution to be paid by that district and by each teacher therein who is a member of the retirement system. The retirement fund receives credit for these amounts through an adequate accounting system in the State Department of Education. The district reimburses itself for the amount so deducted on account of its member teachers by deducting and retaining 4 per cent of the salary due such teachers at each payment period.

Thus it is clear that since the local school board deducts from the member teacher's salary the amount which is withheld by the state on account of such member teachers, this amount is no additional expense to the local school system. As a matter of fact, it could be and often is the source of additional revenue, for, while this amount is gradually accumulating throughout a school year, it is not lost to the system until in April or May following the close of the school year in June. Thus, the school system has had the use of the total amount so deducted for nearly a year, and parts thereof for nearly two years. This money properly administered would yield a revenue to the local district.

It is likewise clear that the deduction made from state moneys on account of the district's share toward the retirement fund is a real *expense* to the local school system even though it is not an *expenditure* as now handled. This fact is not being recognized by all school superintendents in the cities visited. Adequate accounting practice requires a clear distinction between these terms. The amount of this expense is offset by a revenue even though the money represented thereby is not actually received by the school system. This also is not universally recognized throughout the state.

Failure to recognize these fundamental distinctions has led to confusion in the preparation of budgets in many of the cities and villages of the state. Budgetary procedure with respect to retirement fund contributions can follow any one of several methods, each producing a perfectly balanced budget. To illustrate this fact three balanced budgets covering the items under discussion are given below. It will be noted that the totals of these budgets differ as to the specific amounts contained therein. From an accounting standpoint, however, each is superior to the one which precedes it.

For the sake of clarity in presenting these balanced budgets showing local contributions for pensions, teachers' salaries, and revenues from the state, a hypothetical situation will be used. It is assumed that a school district will be entitled to receive $19,200 from state moneys during the fiscal year for which the sample budgets are prepared and that the total teachers' salaries, irrespective of retirement payments, will be $100,000 for the year. From this amount 4 per cent or $4,000 will be deducted during the year by the school board for the retirement fund—assuming that all teachers are members—so that only $96,000 will actually be received by these teachers. The district's contribution to the retirement fund will amount to $5,200 (5.2 per cent of total teachers' salaries for the previous year, assuming that the total has not changed). It is evident, therefore, that the retirement fund will receive a total of $9,200 from this district.

Now, if this amount were to be sent direct to the retirement board at Albany, no school board in the state would fail to carry in its budget as a need the $100,000 for teachers' salaries and the $5,200 for the district's contribution to the retirement fund. This amount, however, is not sent to the retirement board by the school district. It is retained in the treasury of the school district, and nearly a year later it will be deducted by the Administrative Division of the State Department of Education from state moneys due the district from the various quotas and grants provided by law. This method of making payments into the retirement fund is very confusing to those schoolmen in the state who are not familiar with modern accounting methods. They do not have a record of disbursing these amounts and therefore fail to realize that an expense is incurred in the transaction.

Hypothetical Sample Budgets

BUDGET A

ESTIMATED REVENUES		ESTIMATED NEEDS	
Sources:			
Net amount to be received from state	$10,000*	Teachers' salaries	$96,000
Local taxation (to balance budget)	86,000	District's contribution to retirement fund	....
Total revenues	$96,000	Total needs	$96,000

* $19,200 State aid less $9,200 due the retirement fund from this district.

This is a receipt expenditure budget, taking account only of the actual moneys received or disbursed for the items under discussion. While this is a mathematically correct budget, it does not reveal the true state of the financial transactions involved for it makes no provision for the teachers' retirement fund expense item, and the expense item "Teachers' salaries" is $4,000 short. On the revenue side, the state is not credited with its full contribution toward meeting local needs.

BUDGET B

ESTIMATED REVENUES		ESTIMATED NEEDS	
Sources:			
Net amount to be received from state	$ 10,000*		
4 per cent of teachers' salaries to be retained by district	4,000	Teachers' salaries	$100,000
Local taxation (to balance budget)	86,000	District's contribution to retirement fund	....
Total revenues	$100,000	Total needs	$100,000

* See footnote, Budget A.

This is a more complete budget than the preceding one. The amount for teachers' salaries is correct but the other expense item is omitted as it was in Budget A. The criticism of the revenue side of Budget A holds for this budget also. The $4,000 to be retained from teachers' salaries, while in no sense a receipt, has been entered as an estimated revenue in order to balance the budget.

ESTIMATED REVENUES	ESTIMATED NEEDS
Sources:	
State moneys due the district .... $ 19,200	Teachers' salaries $100,000
Local taxation (to balance the budget) 86,000	District's contribution to retirement fund 5,200
Total revenues $105,200	Total needs $105,200

This is a simple revenue-expense budget, accurately and completely representing the true financial situation. To be sure the $19,200 will not be a receipt from the state under the present method of handling retirement fund contributions, but neither will the $5,200 nor the $4,000 of the $100,000 be disbursements. However, both of these last amounts represent expenses to be borne by the school district and should be carried in the budget. Budget C conforms to sound budgetary practices with regard to the items under discussion.

It should be noticed that in every case shown the amount to be raised by local taxation is the same. This is obviously necessary if they are all honest budgets. If, for instance, in Budget B the $4,000 to be deducted from the teachers' salaries had not been entered as an estimated receipt, it would have been necessary to raise $90,000 by local taxation to balance the budget. This amount would have been $4,000 more than actual needs required.

Present Practice in Budgeting for Teachers' Retirement Fund

The above sample budgets including the items, teachers' salaries, local contribution to the teachers' retirement fund, revenues due the local district from the state, and revenues from local taxation, have been given that they might serve as a background for the presentation of present practice within the state in budgeting these items. The hypothetical situation upon which each of these budgets has been based was taken in order to emphasize the principles of sound budgetary procedure and to avoid the confusion which would result if the actual amounts carried in the budgets for these items in the several cities and villages of the state were considered.

TABLE IX

PROCEDURE BEING FOLLOWED BY SCHOOL BOARDS IN FOURTEEN CITIES
AND TWO VILLAGES IN BUDGETING FOR THE STATE TEACHERS' RETIREMENT
FUND AND STATE MONEYS

CITIES AND VILLAGES	EXPENSE ITEMS				REVENUE ITEMS			
	Teachers' Salaries Are Carried in Budget		District's Share of Pension Is Carried in Budget		State Moneys Are Carried in Budget		4 Per Cent to be Deducted from Teachers' Salaries for Retirement Fund Is in Budget	
	Gross	Net	Yes	No	Gross	Net	Yes	No
Cities								
Auburn	x		x		x			x
Batavia	x		x		x			x
Canandaigua	x		x		x			x
Cohoes	x		x		x			x
Elmira	x		x		x			x
Fulton	x		x		x			x
Hornell	x		x		x			x
Lockport	x		x		x			x
Mechanicville	x		x		x			x
Mount Vernon	x		x		x			x
Olean	x		x		x			x
Poughkeepsie	x		x		x			x
Rochester	x		x		x			x
Syracuse	x		x		x			x
Villages								
Hempstead	x		x		x			x
Seneca Falls	x		x		x			x
Number of Cities and Villages	16	0	16	0	16	0	0	16

How to Read Table IX: In the 16 cities of Table IX, the item in the school budget for teachers' salaries is for the full amount of the contracts made or to be made. The district's contribution to the state retirement fund is also included as a need. On the revenue side of the budget is carried the total amount of state moneys to be due the district on account of all quotas or payments provided. No entry is made concerning the amount to be deducted from the teachers' salaries for the retirement fund.

In the fourteen cities and two villages shown in Table IX those responsible for making up the budget are following sound budgetary principles in its preparation covering the items under discussion. In these cities and villages the state is given full credit for all funds due the local district from state-aid grants and quotas provided by law. The entire expense of teachers' salaries is shown in the budget together with the expense incurred by the

TABLE X

PROCEDURE BEING FOLLOWED BY SCHOOL BOARDS IN SIX CITIES IN
BUDGETING FOR THE STATE TEACHERS' RETIREMENT FUND AND STATE
MONEYS

	EXPENSE ITEMS				REVENUE ITEMS			
CITIES	Teachers' Salaries Are Carried in Budget		District's Share of Pension Is Carried in Budget		State Moneys Are Carried in Budget		4 Per Cent to be Deducted from Teachers' Salaries for Retirement Fund Is in Budget	
	Gross	Net	Yes	No	Gross	Net	Yes	No
Albany	x			x		x	x	
Norwich	x			x		x	x	
Saratoga Springs	x			x		x	x	
Troy	x			x		x	x	
Utica	x			x		x	x	
Watervliet	x			x		x	x	
Number of Cities	6	0	0	6	0	6	6	0

How to Read Table X: In the 6 cities of Table X, the item in the school budget for teachers' salaries is for the full amount of the contracts made or to be made. The district's contribution to the state retirement fund is not carried in the budget. On the revenue side of the budget is carried the net amount anticipated from state moneys after deductions have been made for all contributions due the state retirement fund from the district. However, the amount which the local district will deduct from the teachers' salaries as their contributions to the retirement fund is carried as a revenue in the budget.

local district's contribution to the teachers' retirement fund. Since these items are carried in this way no entry need be made covering the teachers' contribution to the retirement fund. In these cities and villages the items under discussion are budgeted as illustrated in sample Budget C on page 32.

In the six cities shown in Table X, budgetary procedure with respect to the items under discussion is not as commendable as that followed by the cities and villages in Table IX. In these six cities the budget does not give the state credit for the full amount of money which is actually received from state-aid grants and quotas. These cities also fail to provide in their budgets for the expense incurred by the local contribution to the teachers' retirement fund. However, they are to be commended for providing for the entire expense of teachers' salaries. Under the circumstances they are also to be commended for considering the amount to be deducted from teachers' salaries

TABLE XI

Procedure Being Followed by the School Boards of Three Cities
in Budgeting for the State Teachers' Retirement Fund and State
Moneys

CITIES	EXPENSE ITEMS				REVENUE ITEMS			
	Teachers' Salaries Are Carried in Budget		District's Share of Pension Is Carried in Budget		State Moneys Are Carried in Budget		4 Per Cent to be Deducted from Teachers' Salaries for Retirement Fund Is in Budget	
	Gross	Net	Yes	No	Gross	Net	Yes	No
Jamestown		x		x		x		x
Oswego		x		x		x		x
Tonawanda		x		x		x		x
Number of Cities	0	3	0	3	0	3	0	3

How to Read Table XI: In the 3 cities of Table XI, the item in the school budget for teachers' salaries is the amount which will actually be received by the teachers, i.e. (contract amount less pension payments). The district's contribution to the retirement fund is not carried in the budget. On the revenue side of the budget, the net amount of state moneys to be received (as in Table X) is carried, but the amount to be deducted from the teachers' salaries before payment is made is not carried.

as an estimated revenue. While in no sense a revenue to the school system, failure to consider it as a revenue, under the present method of budgeting the other items under discussion, would constitute an unsavory practice. This latter practice is being followed by the cities and villages shown in Table XII on page 36. The cities in Table X are following the procedure illustrated in sample Budget B on page 31.

The three cities in Table XI are following the procedure illustrated in sample Budget A on page 31. This procedure is less satisfactory than that found in the cities of either of the two previous groups. The criticisms given above also hold for these cities, but there is nothing for which to commend them. Both of the last two groups would improve their procedure if they changed to that followed by the cities in Table IX as illustrated in sample Budget C on page 32.

TABLE XII

PROCEDURE BEING FOLLOWED BY THE SCHOOL BOARDS IN SIXTEEN CITIES
AND THREE VILLAGES IN BUDGETING FOR THE STATE TEACHERS' RETIRE-
MENT FUND AND STATE MONEYS

CITIES AND VILLAGES	EXPENSE ITEMS				REVENUE ITEMS			
	Teachers' Salaries Are Carried in Budget		District's Share of Pension Is Carried in Budget		State Moneys Are Carried in Budget		4 Per Cent to be Deducted from Teachers' Salaries for Retirement Fund Is in Budget	
	Gross	Net	Yes	No	Gross	Net	Yes	No
Cities								
Amsterdam	x			x		x		x
Corning	x			x		x		x
Dunkirk	x			x		x		x
Glen Cove	x			x		x		x
Gloversville	x			x		x		x
Hudson	x			x		x		x
Johnstown	x			x		x		x
Lackawanna	x			x		x		x
Little Falls	x			x		x		x
New Rochelle	x			x		x		x
Niagara Falls	x			x		x		x
North Tonawanda	x			x		x		x
Oneida	x			x		x		x
Oneonta	x			x		x		x
Rome	x			x		x		x
White Plains	x			x		x		x
Villages								
Herkimer	x			x		x		x
Ilion	x			x		x		x
Lynbrook	x			x		x		x
Number of Cities and Villages	19	0	0	19	0	19	0	19

How to Read Table XII: The 16 cities and 3 villages in Table XII are following the same procedure as those in Table X, except that they are not carrying as an estimated revenue the amount of money which will be deducted from the teachers' salaries for the retirement fund.

Turning to Table XII, sixteen cities and three villages are revealed about which no word of commendation can be said relative to their procedures with respect to the subject under discussion. The budgets which are being prepared in these cities are being padded by means of their methods of budgeting for teachers' salaries, pension contributions, and state moneys. By carrying the gross figure for teachers' salaries on the expenditure side and oñly the net receipts (total state moneys due less amount to be deducted for retirement fund) on the revenue side, they are padding their budgets to the extent of 4 per cent of the member teachers' salaries during the current year. Using the hypothetical situation discussed at some length earlier in this chapter, the illustration below shows how this is being done.

BUDGET D

ESTIMATED REVENUES		ESTIMATED NEEDS	
Sources:			
Net amount to be received from state	$ 10,000*	Teachers' salaries	$100,000
Local taxation (to balance budget)	90,000	District's contribution to retirement fund	....
Total receipts	$100,000	Total needs	$100,000

* See note, Budget A, p. 31.

It should be noted that by this procedure it is necessary to raise $90,000 by local taxation to balance the budget. Thus $100,000 is entered as a need, but only $96,000 of this will actually be expended for teachers' salaries. The $4,000 deducted from the salary checks of the teachers will still remain in the hands of the local school board, since that amount added to the district's contribution to the retirement fund equals the $9,200 to be deducted by the state department. Thus, the local board will receive $14,000 besides the $90,000 from taxation. It is therefore evident that the school board has raised $4,000 more by local taxation than was needed to balance the budget had it been properly prepared. Because the present method of forwarding state moneys after deducting these retirement fund contributions therefrom is so confusing to the men in the field, probably accounts for the fact that these practices are being followed by so many school superintendents in the state.

Several of these superintendents admit using this device to pad their budgets. Their purpose is to "get by" the municipal reviewing authority. If that authority "cuts" the budget, this extra hidden amount will tend to equalize the amount so deducted. Evidence points to the fact that other devices have been used for the same purpose. Such practices are not commendable, but the fact that a superintendent feels called upon to exercise them in order to get the money with which to furnish the kind of educational opportunities to which children are entitled is a strong argument for the removal of the control now exercised over school revenues by municipal authorities.

Recommendation for Collecting Contributions. Many superintendents throughout the state are opposed to the present method of collecting retirement contributions. Many prefer to send the payments direct to the retirement board. If this were done monthly, as provided in the law, it would doubtless occasion too great a clerical expense in the retirement fund office. An annual payment in June or July, however, should not occasion a greater burden on the retirement board than is now felt in the statistical bureau. Much would be accomplished by such an annual direct payment to the retirement board, thereby simplifying budgetary and accounting procedure in the various districts of the state. Besides, the retirement fund is now losing nearly a year's interest on these moneys. The teachers should have the benefit of this interest. Some such plan as suggested above would be beneficial to all concerned. In case any district failed to remit voluntarily, future state moneys should be withheld until all payments are made.

ESTIMATED REVENUES

One measure of the efficiency of budgetary control is the accuracy with which estimates of revenues to be received are made. If estimates are too high for a given period, expenditures must be curtailed or loans must be made to cover the shortage. If estimates are too low, extra money will be available. The latter situation is, of course, preferable to the former within reasonable limits. It is manifestly impossible to estimate anticipated revenues accurately. Apparently no one has scientifically determined the reasonable limits within which the fluctuation should remain. However, Buck[10], an authority on municipal and state finance and budgetary procedure, has set up the following criterion:

The estimate of revenues from sources other than the general property tax should not be more than 10 per cent above or below the actual collections. An estimate that falls far below or greatly exceeds collections of such revenues is either carelessly or intentionally made.

[10] Buck, A. E. *Municipal Budgets and Budget Making* (out of print), p. 37. National Municipal League. New York City, 1925.

TABLE XIII

A COMPARISON BETWEEN ESTIMATED AND ACTUAL RECEIPTS, FROM SOURCES OTHER THAN LOCAL TAXES, OF THE SCHOOL SYSTEMS IN THIRTY-FOUR CITIES AND SIX VILLAGES DURING THE LAST COMPLETED FISCAL YEAR

	1	2	3
CITIES AND VILLAGES	ESTIMATED RECEIPTS *	ACTUAL RECEIPTS *	PERCENTAGE ACTUAL IS OF ESTIMATED RECEIPTS
Cities			
Auburn	$ 149,458	$ 178,360	119.34
Batavia	70,251	78,162	111.26
Canandaigua	44,000	60,539	137.59
Cohoes	44,000	44,941	102.14
Dunkirk	63,510	210,101	330.82
Elmira	180,103	253,559	140.79
Fulton	59,691	73,994	123.96
Glen Cove	55,000	60,146	109.36
Glens Falls	42,636	55,835	130.96
Gloversville	71,943	96,031	133.48
Hornell	75,700	75,908	100.28
Hudson	45,950	43,601	94.89
Jamestown	139,360	204,866	147.00
Lackawanna	53,000	86,327	162.88
Little Falls	79,178	80,227	101.32
Lockport	120,721	138,632	114.84
Mechanicville	60,619	68,270	112.62
Mount Vernon	324,318	343,108	105.79
New Rochelle	156,524	170,607	109.00
North Tonawanda	48,800	54,618	111.92
Olean	125,000	113,515	90.81
Oneida	44,550	39,491	88.64
Oneonta	30,413	51,924	170.73
Oswego	48,000	49,867	103.89
Poughkeepsie	123,018	131,527	106.92
Rochester	1,756,000	1,783,005	101.54
Rome	61,127	63,837	104.43
Saratoga Springs	41,000	37,647	91.82
Schenectady	427,700	435,389	101.80
Syracuse	690,529	689,030	99.78
Troy	149,152	163,397	109.55
Utica	281,020	345,169	122.83
Watervliet	35,429	37,450	105.70
White Plains	155,814	165,568	106.26
Villages			
Hempstead	110,000	144,050	130.96
Herkimer	37,450	38,133	101.82
Ilion	47,850	49,430	103.30
Lynbrook	23,000	112,662	489.84
Peekskill	7,500	55,739	743.19
Seneca Falls	22,250	37,397	168.08

* To the Nearest Dollar.

How to Read Table XIII: In Auburn the school budget for the last completed fiscal year carried estimated receipts amounting to at least $149,458 from sources other than local taxes. Actual receipts from comparable sources during the same period amounted to $178,360 or 119.34 per cent of the amount estimated. This shows that actual receipts from sources other than local taxes were 19.34 per cent above the amount estimated.

In the case of Hudson, actual receipts from sources other than local taxes were 5.11 per cent below the amount estimated.

It was impossible to secure the adequate data necessary for a contrast between estimated and actual revenues in all of the cities included in this study. This was due mainly to laxity in budgetary procedure. In several cities no record was kept of the revenues anticipated during a given period. In some cases the amount of the gross budget from which one could arrive at the desired figure was not even available. Data were obtainable, however, in thirty-four cities and six villages as shown in Table XIII.

Table XIII, column 3, shows the percentage which actual revenues received from sources other than local taxation were of estimated revenues for each city and village in which these data were available. By a cursory glance at this table, one sees great variations in the accuracy with which those responsible for making up the budget estimated revenues for the last completed fiscal year. The application of Buck's[11] criterion to these percentages shows that much greater care or honesty should be practiced by those who are responsible for making up the revenue side of the school budget.

Great care was exercised in making the above figures as comparable as possible before these percentages were figured. The budgetary practices pertaining to state moneys and retirement contributions, discussed at some length earlier in this chapter, could influence this comparison. The comparison made would be even less favorable had not these practices been taken into account. Whenever the budget estimate for state revenues was net, only the amount received was considered as an actual revenue unless the budget item for teachers' salaries was gross. In the latter case, the amount deducted from the salary checks and retained by the school board was considered a revenue in arriving at the total. Another way of expressing this is that, in the cases just mentioned, actual receipts from the state plus deductions from teachers' salaries by the district equaled the figures used as revenues from the state. This would, of course, make the revenues from the state greater than estimated revenues therefrom, provided the estimate was fairly accurate.

Receipts from sale of bonds, temporary loans, or supplies were likewise not included in the total used unless they had been estimated. Whenever any other actual receipt was such that it could not be properly anticipated—such as insurance adjustments—it was omitted in arriving at the total used for that city. In

[11] *Ibid.*

TABLE XIV

A Comparison Between Estimated and Actual Current Expense of the School Systems in Thirty-seven Cities and Six Villages During the Last Completed Fiscal Year

Cities and Villages	1 Amount of Estimated Current Expense *	2 Amount of Actual Current Expense *	3 Percentage Actual Is of Estimated Current Expense
Cities			
Amsterdam	$ 548,875	$ 537,280	97.89
Auburn	432,925	419,853	96.98
Batavia	286,847	282,185	98.38
Beacon	136,710	137,240	100.39
Canandaigua	121,900	119,202	97.79
Cohoes	190,762	181,992	95.40
Dunkirk	430,877	340,952	79.13
Elmira	680,285	625,604	91.96
Fulton	211,691	184,039	86.94
Glen Cove	183,975	159,015	86.43
Glens Falls	201,585	205,081	101.73
Gloversville	348,500	354,053	101.59
Hornell	266,700	295,942	110.96
Hudson	153,200	153,200	100.00
Jamestown	768,834	744,134	96.79
Johnstown	173,795	159,478	91.76
Lackawanna	271,350	257,882	95.04
Little Falls	174,870	158,545	90.66
Lockport	428,581**	441,840**	103.09**
Mechanicville	177,224	179,007	101.01
Mount Vernon	1,332,570	1,301,133	97.64
New Rochelle	1,177,783	1,177,167	99.95
North Tonawanda	253,870	251,978	99.26
Olean	400,200	402,513	100.58
Oneida	154,410	155,001	100.38
Oneonta	168,243	170,495	101.34
Oswego	291,000	291,645	100.22
Poughkeepsie	528,018	544,182	103.06
Rochester	6,535,000	6,400,898	97.95
Rome	331,012	330,988	99.99
Saratoga Springs	183,306	179,416	97.88
Schenectady	1,824,468	1,804,823	98.92
Syracuse	2,624,836	2,585,585	98.50
Troy	684,565	681,704	99.58
Utica	1,426,195	1,414,686	99.19
Watervliet	161,515	161,777	100.16
White Plains	774,841	772,827	99.74
Villages			
Hempstead	290,599	323,762	111.41
Herkimer	141,075	145,431	103.09
Ilion	148,177	145,789	98.39
Lynbrook	152,850	145,360	95.10
Peekskill	190,114	237,794	125.08
Seneca Falls	86,975	90,601	104.17

* To the nearest Dollar.

** Includes capital outlay and debt service.

How to Read Table XIV: In Amsterdam, estimated current expense for the last completed fiscal year was $548,875, and the actual expenditures for like services and period amount to $537,280 or 97.89 per cent of that estimated. This shows that actual current expense was 2.11 per cent below the estimated amount.

In the case of Beacon, actual current expense was 0.39 per cent above the estimated amount for these services.

view of these adjustments, it seems only fair to conclude that those responsible for estimating revenues are not even approximating the accuracy expected in adequate budgetary procedure. In most cases the estimates were too low. In many cases, this was due to failure to include as an estimated revenue the cash balances which were to be on hand at the end of the year. Often the actual balance was too small to affect the comparison, but in other cases the effect was marked. Revenues from many other sources were not anticipated in the budget.

Estimated Expenditures for Current Expense

Another measure of the efficiency of budgetary control is the accuracy with which expenditures are estimated.

Table XIV sets forth the results of such a comparison in the cities and villages which could supply the necessary data for such a test. Sometimes the gross budget was not available. In one city no budget could be found, and in others complete data were not procurable for various reasons. A glance at the table shows that in this phase of budget estimating, those responsible for the budget were much more proficient than in estimating revenues. Expenditures for current expense were less than the estimated figure in a majority of the cases. In very few cases did expenditures for current expense greatly exceed the estimate made for the year. As in the comparison made above, whenever the budget did not contain an estimated expenditure for the district's contribution to the retirement fund, the expenditure for that item was not included in the actual current expense figure used for comparative purposes.

How good is the showing made in this aspect of budget control? In the absence of extended research in this field no valid criterion is available with which to evaluate the above findings. However, Professor G. M. Baker, University of Kentucky, has reported some research in this field. In a study made in Grand Rapids, Michigan, he found that over a period of seven years the variation of estimated current expense over actual current expense, or vice versa, ranged from ½ to 4 per cent. Relative to these findings he says [12]:

These variations are approximately the same as those reported by Louisville and they indicate a most commendable management of finances, and have a special significance to cities of this size.

[12] Baker, G. M. "Financial Practices in Cities and Towns below 25,000." *American School Board Journal*, Dec., 1916, p. 20.

According to this standard, most of the cities in the above comparison are to be commended for their management of finance.

SUMMARY

Findings concerning the operation of certain internal controls of income in the cities visited have been shown in this chapter. The budgetary procedures involved in the carrying out of these controls were found to be quite varied. Concerning the preparation of budget estimates, it was found that committee action of the school board is still prominent in such preparation and that in eleven cities the superintendent of schools has no major part in the formulation of budget estimates. Many school systems do not have a complete budget. Fourteen of these cities omit expenditures for either capital outlay or debt service or for both from their budgets. These school boards are both fiscally dependent and independent so that no direct relationship seems to exist between the dependence of the school system and divided authority in budgeting for complete school expenditures.

Budgeting with respect to the Teachers' Retirement Fund was found to be anything but uniform, with considerable variation in the degree of acceptability of such procedures. In sixteen cities and three villages the budget is being padded by the methods in use. Sample budgets covering a hypothetical situtation were presented with recommendations for the improvement of this phase of income control.

A comparison between the estimated receipts from sources other than local taxation and the actual receipts from these sources revealed considerable inaccuracy in this phase of income control. In half the cities and villages for which this comparison could be made, the degree of inaccuracy exceeded the 10 per cent limit which Buck[13] has set up as a measure of the care or honesty which is exercised in estimating these receipts.

A comparison similar to the one above was made between the estimated expenditures for current expenses and the actual expenditures for these services. The result of this comparison was much more favorable than that between estimated and actual revenues. According to Baker's criterion,[14] these officials are to be commended for their management of finances.

[13] See footnote 10, p. 38.
[14] See footnote 12, p. 42.

CHAPTER IV

THE TAX CALENDAR AND THE FISCAL YEAR

INTRODUCTION

Authorities in municipal finance are concerned with the proper coördination of the tax calendar with the fiscal year period. Buck, prominent among these authorities, has written the following on this aspect of municipal finance:[1]

The financial calendar permits a careful adjustment to the fiscal year of the time for the preparation and passage of the budget and the assessment and collection of taxes. Such a calendar may be outlined briefly as follows:

1. Assessment of property begun.
2. Assessment of property completed.
3. Departments begin preparing estimates.
4. Departments finish preparing estimates.
5. Preparation of budget by budget-making authority.
6. Budget submitted to city council.
7. City elections held.
8. Beginning of political year.
9. Discussion of budget and public hearings by the council.
10. Budget adopted by the council and budget ordinance passed.
11. Tax rate fixed.
12. Beginning of fiscal year.
13. Collection of general property taxes.
    (a) First installment
    (b) Second installment

In the largest cities the assessment of property is an all-year-round work. However, property is generally assessed as of a certain date. This date should be some time prior to the beginning of the fiscal year. The collection of property taxes, at least part of such taxes, should come early in the fiscal year in order to finance the work of the city government without having to resort to short-time loans. The date of the beginning of the political year should precede by a short time that of the fiscal year (especially where the chief executive officer is elective as in the case of the mayor—council cities), so as to give the incoming administration an opportunity to make any changes in the budget that may seem necessary before it is finally adopted. The budget made up by the outgoing administration should be published before the election so that any mooted points may be made issues before the people. Then the incoming rather than the outgoing city council should finally adopt the budget.

[1] Buck, A. E. *Municipal Budgets and Budget Making*, p. 72. *op. cit.*

The Special Joint Committee on Taxation and Retrenchment of the New York State Legislature has also touched upon the desirability for proper coördination between the tax calendar and the fiscal year. In its report dealing with retrenchment will be found the following paragraphs :[2]

Many of the cities of the state are paying interest on temporary loans which might be saved if the taxes were collected early enough in the fiscal year to make temporary borrowing unnecessary. In Utica, for example, the taxes are not collected until September for a fiscal year beginning the previous January 1. For two-thirds of the year the city is forced to operate on funds borrowed at a rate of 4 to 5 per cent interest. The cost of this system in Utica for 1919 alone is placed at $20,000. In Syracuse the cost is $50,000. In New York City the controller has stated that the cost is approximately $3,000,000 annually. Mayor Burns told the Committee that Troy had abolished this system by advancing the date of tax collection, thereby saving $42,000 a year. Mayor Cox of Middletown has accomplished an annual saving of $7,000 by the inauguration of the same policy. Schenectady is now in the process of advancing its date of tax collection.

While it has been impossible for this Committee to make a complete estimate of the saving that can be made by advancing the dates of tax collection in the score or more cities that now collect anywhere from three to nine months after the beginning of the fiscal year, an estimate based on payments of 1919 indicates a possible saving of between three and four millions of dollars per year.

In the Report of the Special Joint Committee on Taxation and Retrenchment, New York State Legislature, 1922, page 41, attention was again called to the failure of cities to collect taxes early enough to save interest on temporary loans.

Before taking up the dates of occurrence of the various events in the tax calendar and their relation to the fiscal year period, it will be well to discover who levies and collects school taxes in the various cities of the state. This knowledge, together with the extent to which school taxes are collected simultaneously with city, state, or county taxes, will assist in the interpretation of later findings.

School Tax Levy

From column 1 (b) of Table XV, it is evident that school taxes are being levied by the common council in a majority of the cities studied. In twenty-nine cities the common council levies the school tax, in eleven cities this is done by the school board, and in three cities it is the duty of the board of supervisors. These findings

[2] Legislative Document No. 80, pp. 19-20. J. B. Lyon Co., Albany, 1920.

TABLE XV

OFFICIALS WHO LEVY AND COLLECT SCHOOL TAXES IN FORTY-THREE CITIES AND SEVEN VILLAGES IN NEW YORK STATE

CITIES AND VILLAGES	1 SCHOOL TAXES ARE LEVIED BY			2 SCHOOL TAXES ARE COLLECTED BY		
	(a) School Board	(b) City Council	(c) Supervisors	(a) School Collector	(b) City Collector	(c) Town Collector
Cities						
Albany			X		X	
Amsterdam		X			X	
Auburn		X			X	
Batavia	X			X		
Beacon		X			X	
Canandaigua	X			X		
Cohoes		X			X	
Corning	X				X	
Dunkirk	X				X	
Elmira			X		X	
Fulton		X			X	
Geneva	X				X	
Glen Cove		X			X	
Glens Falls	X				X	
Gloversville		X			X	
Hornell	X				X	
Hudson		X			X	
Jamestown		X			X	
Johnstown		X			X	
Lackawanna	X				X	
Little Falls		X			X	
Lockport		X			X	
Mechanicville	X			X		
Mount Vernon		X			X	
New Rochelle		X			X	
Niagara Falls		X			X	
North Tonawanda	X				X	
Norwich	X				X	
Olean			X	X		
Oneida		X			X	
Oneonta		X			X	
Oswego		X			X	
Poughkeepsie		X			X	
Rochester		X			X	
Rome		X			X	
Saratoga Springs		X			X	
Schenectady		X			X	
Syracuse		X			X	
Tonawanda		X			X	
Troy		X			X	
Utica		X			X	
Watervliet		X			X	
White Plains		X			X	
Total Cities	11	29	3	4	39	
Villages						
Green Island	X			X		
Hempstead			X			X
Herkimer	X			X		
Ilion	X			X		
Lynbrook			X			X
Peekskill	X					X
Seneca Falls	X				X	
Total Villages	5	0	2	3	1	3
Grand Total	16	29	5	7	40	3

How to Read Table XV: In Albany, school taxes are levied by the board of supervisors and collected by the city tax receiver.

are in distinct contrast to the method of levying of taxes in the city school systems of the State of Pennsylvania, where all school taxes are levied by the board of school directors. In the village school districts of New York State, the school board usually levies the tax for school purposes. In Nassau County the school board of each village notifies the board of supervisors as to the amount of its school budget. This amount is then levied by the latter board and collected by the tax collector of the town in which the village is located.

SCHOOL TAX COLLECTION

Collection Official

Column 2 (b) of Table XV shows that in thirty-nine of the forty-three cities studied school taxes are collected by the city tax receiver. In two of the four cities shown as having this tax collected by the school board, the clerk of the board acts as tax receiver in addition to his other duties. In the other two, a school tax collector is engaged by the school board. In one of these latter two cities the school board is anxious to have the city chamberlain collect school taxes. This will doubtless be arranged as soon as circumstances warrant.

In some of these cities the school board pays part of the city tax receiver's salary. In others a collection fee, which goes into the city treasury, is added to the tax. This fee, usually 1 per cent during the first month and 5 per cent thereafter, returns to the city a sum out of all proportion to the service rendered by that city official, who, in turn, usually gets no additional compensation for the extra work involved. In some of these cities the school board not only pays nothing for this service but the expense of stationery and billing taxes is borne by the city. It seems but fair that the school board should pay the city for the additional trouble and expense caused by this service for the schools. If this were equitably done and the proper official received the benefit thereof, there would be less ill feeling on the part of these individuals for having to perform this extra service. The advantages to all concerned of having the city tax receiver collect all tax moneys are so great that school taxes should be collected by that individual after a sound, equitable arrangement has been made.

TABLE XVI

How Taxes Were Collected in 1917 and in 1927 in Forty-three Cities and Seven Villages in New York State

	1		2		3		4	
Cities and Villages	School Tax Collected Separately		City Tax Collected with School Tax		State and County Tax Collected with School Tax		State, County, and City Tax Collected with School Tax	
	1917(a)	1927(b)	1917(a)	1927(b)	1917(a)	1927(b)	1917(a)	1927(b)
Cities								
Albany	X							X
Amsterdam			X	X				
Auburn		X					X	
* Batavia		X						
Beacon							X	X
Canandaigua	X	X						
Cohoes							X	X
Corning	X	X						
* Dunkirk						X		
Elmira						X	X	
Fulton		X					X	
Geneva	X	X						
* Glen Cove								X
Glens Falls					X	X		
Gloversville	X	X						
Hornell	X	X						
Hudson							X	X
* Jamestown		X						
Johnstown	X	X						
Lackawanna	X	X						
Little Falls			X			X		
* Lockport		X						
Mechanicville	X	X						
Mount Vernon							X	X
New Rochelle							X	X
Niagara Falls		X					X	
North Tonawanda			X	X				
Norwich	X	X						
Olean	X	X						
Oneida							X	X
Oneonta	X	X						
Oswego			X	X				
Poughkeepsie			X	X				
Rochester			X	X				
Rome			X					X
Saratoga Springs							X	X
Schenectady							X	X
Syracuse			X	X				
* Tonawanda				X				
Troy							X	X
Utica			X	X				
Watervliet							X	X
White Plains							X	X
Villages *								
Green Island		X						
Hempstead						X		
Herkimer		X						
Ilion		X						
Lynbrook						X		
Peekskill		X						
Seneca Falls		X						
Grand Total	12	22	9	8	1	6	15	14

* Not included in 1917 study.

a As shown by Report No. 303, *How and When Taxes are Collected in New York Cities.* New York State Bureau of Municipal Information, Dec. 14, 1917.

b From data personally gathered by the writer.

How to Read Table XVI: In Albany school taxes were being collected separate from all other taxes in 1917, but in 1927 they were being collected with state, county, and city taxes.

Combined Tax Collection

Changes During Ten-Year Period. In Table XVI is shown a comparison of the various combinations in which school taxes were being collected in 1917 and in 1927. This table shows that a number of changes have occurred in the last ten years with respect to combining school tax collection with the collection of other taxes. In eight of the cities for which data could be obtained covering this point a change in procedure is recorded. A careful analysis of these changes fails to reveal any distinct trend. It should be noted, however, that in three cities now collecting school taxes separately these taxes were being collected with other taxes in 1917, while the reverse is true in only one city. This indicates that there has been a slight trend toward collection of school taxes separate from other taxes in the cities included in this analysis.

Cities Grouped According to Combination. In order that a clearer concept may be formed of the number and identity of the cities in which the collection of school taxes is now combined with the collection of other local taxes, Table XVII is inserted at this point. A consideration of these groupings has been postponed until an analysis has been made of the findings relative to the dates when the various events in the tax calendar occurred.

COÖRDINATION OF THE TAX CALENDAR AND THE FISCAL YEAR

Recalling the statements of experts in municipal finance as given in the introduction to this chapter, one interested in school finance naturally asks the question: To what extent is the collection of school taxes coördinated with the school fiscal year? This question is one which should receive the attention of those responsible for determining the various dates in the school financial calendar.

The Situation in Cities in Other States

An effort was made to discover this relationship in other states than New York. Correspondence with officials in many State Departments of Education disclosed the fact that in most of these states no study has been made which brings into relief the time relationship existing between the dates when school taxes are collected and the beginning of the school fiscal year in the cities

TABLE XVII

CITIES AND VILLAGES OF THIS STUDY IN WHICH SCHOOL TAXES ARE COLLECTED SEPARATELY OR WITH OTHER TAXES

SCHOOL TAXES ARE BEING COLLECTED SEPARATELY IN	SCHOOL TAXES ARE BEING COLLECTED WITH CITY TAXES IN	SCHOOL TAXES ARE BEING COLLECTED WITH STATE AND COUNTY TAXES IN	SCHOOL TAXES ARE BEING COLLECTED WITH STATE, COUNTY, AND CITY TAXES IN
Cities	Cities	Cities	Cities
Auburn	Amsterdam	Dunkirk	Albany
Batavia	North Tonawanda	Elmira	Beacon
Canandaigua	Oswego	Glens Falls	Cohoes
Corning	Rochester	Little Falls	Glen Cove
Fulton	Schenectady		Hudson
Geneva	Syracuse	Villages	Mount Vernon
Gloversville	Tonawanda	Hempstead	New Rochelle
Hornell	Utica	Lynbrook	Oneida
Jamestown			Poughkeepsie
Johnstown			Rome
Lackawanna			Saratoga Springs
Lockport			Troy
Mechanicville			Watervliet
Niagara Falls			White Plains
Norwich			
Olean			
Oneonta			
Villages			
Green Island			
Herkimer			
Ilion			
Peekskill			
Seneca Falls			

of those states.   Nor does any publication give the dates of occurrence of the various events in the school tax calendar of the cities in those states.   By means of this correspondence and the study of school laws, however, it was discovered that, in several states, school tax collection dates are either the same in all the cities of a state or in all the cities of the same class therein.   Missouri is an example of the former type of uniformity, and Pennsylvania is an example of the latter.   In Missouri:[3]

The tax list is made up by assessors in June and the tax is paid on this assessment one year from the following December.   This is a state law and applies to all cities and school districts in Missouri.   The school fiscal year begins July 1, and ends June 30.   Assessments made June, 1925, are paid December, 1926, and so on.   Therefore, 1926 taxes are available to pay any school expenditure after January 1, 1927, and so on.

[3] Quoted from a letter to the writer from George W. Reavis, Assistant Executive Officer State Department of Education, Jefferson City, Mo.

It is evident that in Missouri schools have been in session at least three months before tax moneys for expenditures during those months have been received. The fiscal year is nearly half gone when these moneys are collected.

In Pennsylvania cities, the school directors levy and assess all school taxes.[4] In the first-class cities, whose school fiscal year begins January 1,[5] these taxes are collected at the same time and manner as other city taxes.[6] In second-, third-, or fourth-class cities the tax duplicate and the proper warrant must be furnished the tax collector on or before the first Monday of July in each year.[7] In second-class cities a 1 per cent rebate is allowed if the tax is paid before August 1, and in these cities as well as in third- and fourth-class cities a penalty is added to all taxes not paid before the first day of October.[8] Thus it appears that in Pennsylvania cities school moneys from local taxation are available when they are needed to meet school expenditures.

In certain states, Delaware for example, the city school systems are not dependent upon the collection of local taxes for the operation of their schools. The legislature in such states appropriates the money necessary for the operation of schools directly to the various school systems from funds at its disposal. These amounts are made available as needed.[9]

The Situation in Cities in New York State

In order to discover the degree of coördination of the tax calendar with the fiscal year in the school systems of New York State, several officials in the State Department of Education and in the State Tax Department at Albany were interviewed when this study was first contemplated. However, the desired objective data were not available in either of these departments. In the Statistical Division of the State Tax Department it was learned that data with which to show this coördination for state, county, and city taxes were then being prepared for publication.[10] Data on school taxes, however, had not been asked for in the question-

[4] *The School Law*, Secs. 524 and 537. Harrisburg, Pa., 1923.
[5] *Ibid.* Sec. 523.
[6] *Ibid.* Sec. 527.
[7] *Ibid.* Sec. 549.
[8] *Ibid.* Sec. 561.
[9] Personal letter from James O. Adams, Business Manager, State Department of Education, Dover, Delaware.
[10] These data have since been published in Table 28 of the Annual Report of the State Tax Commission, 1925. Legislative Document (1926) No. 7. pp. 119ff.

TABLE XVIII

THE NUMBER OF DAYS WHICH ELAPSED BETWEEN THE BEGINNING OF THE SCHOOL FISCAL YEAR AND THE DATE WHEN CERTAIN EVENTS IN THE TAX CALENDAR OF THE LAST COMPLETED FISCAL YEAR OCCURRED

REFERENCE NUMBER FOR FOLLOWING TABLES	CITIES AND VILLAGES	1 A +	2 DAYS FROM A TO B + (a)	3 DAYS FROM A TO C + (a)	4 DAYS FROM A TO D + (a)	5 DAYS FROM A TO E + (a)	6 DAYS FROM A TO F + (a)	7 DAYS FROM A TO G + (a)	8 DAYS FROM A TO H + (a)
	CITIES								
1	Albany	Jan. 1	−73	−25	−43	−24	−3	0	90
2	Amsterdam	Aug. 1	−129	−116	0	1	18	23	53
3	Auburn	Aug. 1	−82	−74	−61			31	61
4	Batavia	Aug. 1	−7	3	−40	44	58	58	88
5	Beacon	Jan. 1	−101	−12	−93	−93	29	31	61
6	Canandaigua	Aug. 1	−106	−88	−45	45	61	65	65
7	Cohoes	Jan. 1	−11	47	−108	47	48	59	79
8	Corning	Aug. 1	30	30	0	0	30	100	100
9	Dunkirk	Aug. 1	9	9	19	45	163	163	163
10	Elmira	Jan. 1	−95	−58	−92	−17	1	1	31
11	Fulton	Jan. 1	−64	−14	−121	7	148	148	178
12	Geneva	Aug. 1	−92	−88	31	61	105	105	105
13	Glen Cove	Jan. 1	−86	−80	−113		46	−31	9
14	Glens Falls	Aug. 1	−120	−88	−109	−73	−177	177	197
15	Gloversville	Aug. 1	−162	−153	−194	−188	−139	31	61
16	Hornell	May 1	16	16	45	45	53	53	83
17	Hudson	Aug. 1	−200	−162	−213	−151	−120	−89	59
18	Jamestown	Aug. 1	−89	−89	114	125	177	177	207
19	Johnstown	Aug. 1	37	31	20	29	38	39	69
20	Lackawanna	Aug. 1	−4	3	−31	6	59	61	101
21	Little Falls	Jan. 1	67	104	−104	106	119	120	150
22	Lockport	Jan. 1	−217	−172	−190	−165	−115	0	30
23	Mechanicville	Aug. 1	−8	4			44	44	44
24	Mount Vernon	Jan. 1	−66	−38	−133	−37	4	0	30
25	New Rochelle	Jan. 1	19	74	4	72	81	86	116
26	Niagara Falls	Aug. 1	−155	−136	−153	−144	−103	61	31
27	North Tonawanda	Aug. 1	−24	3	12	4	30	31	61
28	Norwich	Aug. 1	89	−88	19	45	60	61	61
29	Olean	Aug. 1	−100	−88	−122	88	0	0	0
30	Oneida	Jan. 1	−86	−86	−103	17	12	17	47
31	Oneonta	Aug. 1	−25	−17	−286	12	9	31	61
32	Oswego	Jan. 1	109	181	181	185	207	212	242
33	Poughkeepsie	Jan. 1	−99	−62	−114	47	14	14	44
34	Rochester	Jan. 1	−2	67	−20	90	90	120	150
35	Rome	Jan. 1	−88	−74	−79	68	−1	0	30

No.	Municipality	A	B	C	D	E	F	G	H
36	Saratoga Springs	Jan. 1	−98	−63	−124	−52	−1	−11	41
37	Schenectady	Jan. 1	−78	−58	−1	−14	−73	90	120
38	Syracuse	Jan. 1	−45	−73	−88	−96	−134	151	181
39	Tonawanda	Jan. 1	−117	−89	−69	−68	−37	−37	—
40	Troy	Jan. 1	−78	−14	−129	−14	−14	0	30
41	Utica	Jan. 1	−63	−75	−93	−76	168	220	250
42	Watervliet	Jan. 1	−23	−14	−91	−3	−7	−8	38
43	White Plains	Jan. 1	−161	−73	−122	−73	−31	−1	31
	Number of Cases	1	43	43	42	40	42	43	43
	Range		−217 to 109	−172 to 181	−286 to 181	−188 to 185	−139 to 207	−89 to 220	−59 to 250
	Median		−78.8	−38	−65	−1	30	31.9	61.8
	VILLAGES								
1V	Green Island	Aug. 1	−92	−88	−39	39	43	43	43
2V	Hempstead	July 1	−77	−57	22	71	147	153	193
3V	Herkimer	Aug. 1	−31	10	45	62	80	80	80
4V	Ilion	Aug. 1	−61	−3	24	24	34	34	34
5V	Lynbrook	Aug. 1	−120	−88	−53	−31	116	122	162
6V	Peekskill	Aug. 1	−95	−88	−407	−78	20	31	61
7V	Seneca Falls	Aug. 1	−94	−81	17	33	54	58	58
	Number of Cases	1	7	7	7	7	7	7	7
	Range		−120 to −31	−88 to 10	−407 to 45	−78 to 71	20 to 147	31 to 153	34 to 193
	Median		−92	−81	17	33	54	58	61
	CITIES AND VILLAGES COMBINED								
	Cases	1	50	50	49	47	49	50	50
	Range		−217 to 109	−172 to 181	−407 to 181	−188 to 185	−139 to 207	−89 to 220	−59 to 250
	Median		−78.8	−57.5	−43	6	38	41	61.7

+ Events in tax calendar.

(a) A minus sign preceding a number indicates that the second event symbolized by the letters at the head of the columns occurred before the first event.

A. Date when school fiscal year began.
B. Date when budget was adopted by school board.
C. Date when budget was finally adopted by reviewing authority.
D. Date assessment roll was completed.
E. Date tax rate was determined.
F. Date the tax warrant was signed.
G. Date tax collection began.
H. Date penalties were added for late payment.

How to Read Table XVIII: In Albany, where the school fiscal year begins Jan. 1, the school budget for the fiscal year beginning Jan. 1, 1926 was adopted by the school board 73 days before Jan. 1. The school budget was adopted by the final reviewing authority 25 days before Jan. 1. The assessment roll was completed 43 days before Jan. 1 and the tax rate was fixed 24 days before Jan. 1. The tax warrant was signed 3 days before Jan. 1, and tax collection began 0 days after Jan. 1. Penalties were added to uncollected taxes 90 days after Jan. 1.

naire by which the above data were procured. The director of that division plans to seek data on school taxes in subsequent studies made by his staff.

Inasmuch as the original data were not available from which an analysis could be made, it was necessary to seek these in the cities and villages to be visited. This phase of the present study must, therefore, be confined to those cities in which the necessary data could be secured.

In the analysis referred to on page 49, relative to the dates when the various events in the tax calendar occurred in the New York cities included in this study, the dates of eight major events have been considered. These dates,[11] with the letters which are used later in their stead, are:

A. Date when the school fiscal year began.

B. Date when the budget was adopted by the school board.

C. Date when the budget was finally approved by the reviewing authority.

D. Date the assessment roll was completed.

E. Date the tax rate was determined.

F. Date the tax warrant was signed.

G. Date that tax collection began.

H. Date when penalties were added for late payment of taxes.

Technique Used for Comparisons. The mere recording of the dates when the above events took place would not assist greatly in discovering the relationship which was being investigated. Hence, it was not followed. Instead, the date when each of these events occurred was referred to the date when the fiscal year began in the school system considered. The number of days intervening between the date when an event occurred and the date when the fiscal year began was used as the measure for comparison with a like measure in another city for the same event. In this way it was possible to make comparisons between the dates of occurrence of similar or dissimilar events regardless of the date when the fiscal year began.

This alone was not adequate, however, for a valid measure should enable one to make a distinction between an event which occurred a given number of days before the fiscal year began and one which occurred the same number of days after the fiscal year

11 See Chap. I, p. 4, for an explanation of the year in which these events occurred.

began. In order to satisfy this requirement, the above measure was considered negative if the event occurred before the fiscal year began, and positive if it occurred afterward. When no negative sign precedes this measure in the following tables it should be considered positive. The use of this refined measure made the further consideration of the actual dates of occurrence of these events in the various cities and villages unnecessary. This refined measure as computed for each event in each city and village is shown in Table XVIII. These measures also furnish the basic data for later tables.

Analysis of Data. Now that the data with which to discover the time relationship existing between the tax calendar and the fiscal year could be placed in convenient form for analysis, the first event considered was that of tax collection. The opinions of authorities in municipal finance concerning the proper occurrence of this event in relation to the beginning of the fiscal year have been noted above. From Table XVIII the situation in the cities included in this phase of the present study is discernible.

Column 7 of Table XVIII shows that in one of these cities school taxes were collected eighty-nine days before the fiscal year began, and in another two hundred and twenty days afterward. The other cities are well scattered between these two extremes. In four cities tax collection began before the fiscal year started; in six cities it began the same day as the fiscal year; and in the remaining thirty-three cities and seven villages it began subsequent thereto. In half of these cities and villages tax collection began less than forty-one days after the fiscal year began, and in the other half it began more than forty-one days after that date. In the group of forty-three cities, the median city began its tax collection 31.9 days after the opening of the fiscal year.

Submission and Testing of Hypotheses.

The question as to why there is this great variance in the occurrence of this important event in the school systems studied immediately presents itself. Many answers to this query can be given, but they must be tested and evaluated in the light of accompanying and subsequent findings before they can be accepted. The relative size of these cities is not an important factor, for in some of the smaller cities tax collection is delayed as long after the beginning of the fiscal year as it is in the larger cities, and in some of the larger cities taxes are collected as early in the fiscal year as in many of the smaller cities. It should be noted that five of the seven remaining events in the comparison shown must take place before these taxes can be collected. Perhaps the occurrence of one or more of these events complicates the situation. Then, too, there is the possibility that the type of external control of income, or the personnel levying and collecting these taxes, or the coincidence of school, city, state, and county tax collection—or the absence of such coincidence—may account for the differences found. To a testing of these hypotheses attention will now be given.

Theoretically the ideal date upon which to begin the collection of taxes is the date when the fiscal year begins due to the fact that expenditures for services and goods during that year may begin at once. However, because less than one-fourth of the cities studied began their collection of taxes that early, it was felt that the ideal date should be replaced by one more practical. From every standpoint a date one full month after the beginning of the fiscal year seemed a fair one, so, for the purposes of comparing and testing the hypotheses enumerated in the last paragraph, these forty-three cities and seven villages were divided into two groups. The first of these two groups, Group I, contains all cities and villages in which tax collection began within thirty-one days after the fiscal year began; Group II contains all those cities and villages in which tax collection began more than thirty-one days after the beginning of the fiscal year. Cities and villages in Group I are shown in Table XIX, and cities and villages in Group II are shown in Table XX. It should be noted that in the median city of Group I tax collection began 1.8 days after the fiscal year began, while in the typical city of Group II it began one hundred and twenty days after the fiscal year began.

Comparison of Cities in Tables XIX and XX.

The basis of this comparison will be the number of days before or after the beginning of the fiscal year that certain events took place in the median city of each group. The median city is taken rather than the mean city because the former measure is less affected by the extreme cities in the group.

As noted above, tax collection is dependent upon five of the seven other events making up the tax calendar under discussion.

These are all sequential with the exception of the assessment roll. It may be completed before or after the budget has been adopted and reviewed, but must be finished before a correct tax rate can be determined. The writer knows of no valid reason why the assessment roll should be completed after the budget has been adopted. There are, however, many valid reasons why it should be completed before the budget is adopted. A sufficient one is that it is highly desirable to know what amount of money the tax rate of a current year will yield for the following year before the budget is adopted. It is obvious that this cannot be known until the assessed valuation for the following year is known. It will be recalled that in the financial calendar[12] quoted from Buck early in this chapter, that authority placed this event ahead of every other event.

A glance down column 6 of Tables XIX and XX, respectively, shows that in only eighteen of these fifty cities and villages was the assessment roll completed before the school budget was adopted by the board of education. The remaining thirty-two school boards had to adopt their budgets without knowing the assessed valuation upon which school taxes were to be raised for the following year. Column 7 of these same tables shows that in only twenty-six cities and one village did the reviewing authorities know the assessed valuation when they put their stamp of approval upon the school budget. Sound business procedure demands that assessed valuations be known before budgets are adopted by local school boards. These findings are similar to those which led the Special Joint Committee on Taxation and Retrenchment, New York State Legislature, to make the following recommendation:[13]

In addition, we urge upon the cities the careful and complete revision of their local assessment and revenue systems.

It should be noted from columns 6 and 7 of Tables XIX and XX that Group I contains the larger number of cities in which the assessment roll is completed before the adoption of the budget by the school board and the reviewing authority. A tax rate cannot be determined accurately until the assessed valuation is known. Since in the median city of Group II the assessment roll was not completed until fifty-six and thirty-two days *after* the school

[12] See footnote 1, p. 44.

[13] Legislative Document, No. 97, p. 19. J. B. Lyon Co., Albany, 1925.

TABLE XIX*

GROUP I CITIES

THE DAY SPAN IS HERE SHOWN BETWEEN CERTAIN EVENTS IN THE SCHOOL TAX CALENDAR OF TWENTY-TWO CITIES AND ONE VILLAGE IN WHICH SCHOOL TAXES WERE COLLECTED AS EARLY AS OR EARLIER THAN THIRTY-ONE DAYS AFTER THE LAST COMPLETED FISCAL YEAR BEGAN

Number of City or Village in Table XVIII	1 Days from A to G +(a)	2 Days from A to B +(a)	3 Days from A to C +(a)	4 Days from B to C +(a)	5 Days from A to A +(a)	6 Days from B to B +(a)	7 Days from C to D +(a)	8 Days from A to E +(a)	9 Days from D to E +	10 Days from A to A +(a)	11 Days from E to F +	12 Days from F to G +	13 Days from C to C +(a)	14 Days from B to G +	15 Days from C to G +	16 Days from G to H +	17 Population in Thousands 1925
17	−89	−200	−162	38	−213	−13	−51	−151	62	−120	31	31	11	111	73	30	12
26	−61	−155	−136	19	−153	2	−17	−144	9	−103	41	42	8	94	75	30	57
39	−31	−117	−89	28	−113	48	−20	−68	1	−37	31	6	21	86	58	30	11
13	−31	−86	−80	48	−43	27	−33	−73	40	−46	27	15	7	55	49	40	11
1		−73	−25	45	−190	30	−18	−24	19	−3	21	3	1	73	25	90	118
22	0	−217	−172	28	−133	27	−18	−165	25	−115	50	115	7	217	172	30	22
24	0	−66	−38	12	−122	67	−95	−37	96	−4	33	4	1	66	38	30	50
29	0	−100	−88	14	−79	22	−34	−88	34	0	88	0	0	100	88	0	21
35	0	−88	−74	64	−129	51	−5	−68	11	−14	67	1	6	88	74	30	72
40	−1	−78	−14	37	−92	39	−115	−14	115	−1	0	14	0	96	14	30	48
10	−8	−95	−14	88	−122	68	−34	−17	75	−14	16	2	41	78	59	30	27
43	−11	−161	−58	9	−91	26	−49	−73	49	−31	42	32	11	162	74	30	16
42	14	−23	−73	35	−124	15	−77	−3	88	−7	10	1	11	31	22	30	14
36	17	−98	−14	37	−114	17	−61	−52	72	−1	51	12	15	109	76	30	36
33	23	−99	−63	0	−103	129	−52	−47	67	−14	29	0	69	113	103	30	11
30	31	−86	−62	13	0	21	−17	−17	86	−12	17	5	117	103	139	30	35
2	31	−129	−116	89	61	8	−116	−1	1	−18	122	73	−81	152	105	30	36
3	31	−82	−74	9	−93	32	−13	−93	0	−29	49	2	35	113	43	30	12
5	31	−101	−12	27	−194	12	−81	−188	6	−139	26	170	1	132	184	30	22
15	31	−162	−153	8	−12		−41	−4	16	−30	21	1	5	193	28	30	17
27		−24	−3		−286	−261	−15	−12	274	−9		22		55	48	30	12
31		−25	−17				−269							56		30	
6V	31	−95	−88	7	−407	−312	−319	−78	329	20	98	11	10	126	119	30	18
Cases	23	23	23	23	23	23	23	23	23	23	23	23	22	23	23	23	23
Range	−89 to 31	−217 to −23	−172 to 3	0 to 89	−407 to 0	−312 to 129	−319 to 116	−188 to 4	0 to 329	−139 to 30	0 to 122	0 to 170	−81 to 117	31 to 217	14 to 184	..	11 to 118
Median	1.8	−95.8	−74.3	27	−114	−13	−34.8	−60	44.5	−1.7	32	6	6.5	100	74.2	..	22.3

* For explanation of references in this table see Table XVIII.

How to read Table XIX: See instructions following Table XX.

board and reviewing authority had adopted the budget, while in the median city of Group I it was completed thirteen and thirty-four days *before* the budget was adopted by these authorities, it appears that the occurrence of this event is a determining factor in the delayed tax collection in the cities of Group II. Other factors which might be influential, however, must be examined before such a conclusion can be accepted.

An inspection of column 14 of Tables XIX and XX brings out the fact that a shorter time elapsed in the cities of Group I, from the date when the budget was adopted by the school board until tax collection began, than in the cities of Group II. In the median city of Group I, this time span was one hundred days, while in the median city of Group II it was one hundred and twenty-two days. The factors which enter into the determination of this time span will now be examined. For simplicity of expression the letters used earlier in the chapter are employed at this point to stand for the date of occurrence of the various events in the tax calendar. For the convenience of the reader they are repeated here:

A. Date when school fiscal year began.
B. Date when budget was adopted by school board.
C. Date when budget was finally approved by reviewing authority.
D. Date assessment roll was completed.
E. Date tax rate was determined.
F. Date tax warrant was signed.
G. Date tax collection began.
H. Date penalties were added for late payment of taxes.

As noted above, the span B to G was one hundred days in length in the median city of Group I, while it was one hundred and twenty-two days in length in the median city in Group II. It is clear that the span from B to G has the component parts B to C, C to D, D to E, E to F, and F to G. Which of these are influential factors favoring the finding in the cities of Group I? Column 4 of Tables XIX and XX shows a twenty-seven-day median span for B to C in Group I cities, while in Group II cities it is a twenty-day span. This, therefore, is not the factor sought. Column 11 of these tables shows a thirty-two-day median span for E to F in Group I cities and in Group II cities it is twenty-one

TABLE XX*

GROUP II CITIES

THE DAY SPAN IS HERE SHOWN BETWEEN CERTAIN EVENTS IN THE SCHOOL TAX CALENDAR OF TWENTY-ONE CITIES AND SIX VILLAGES IN WHICH SCHOOL TAXES WERE COLLECTED LATER THAN THIRTY-ONE DAYS AFTER THE BEGINNING OF THE LAST COMPLETED SCHOOL FISCAL YEAR

NUMBER OF CITY OR VILLAGE IN TABLE XVIII	1 DAYS FROM A to G +	2 DAYS FROM A to B +a	3 DAYS FROM A to C +a	4 DAYS FROM B to C +	5 DAYS FROM A to D +a	6 DAYS FROM B to D +a	7 DAYS FROM C to D +a	8 DAYS FROM A to E +a	9 DAYS FROM D to E +	10 DAYS FROM A to F +	11 DAYS FROM E to F +	12 DAYS FROM F to G +	13 DAYS FROM C to E +a	14 DAYS FROM B to G +	15 DAYS FROM C to G +	16 DAYS FROM G to H +	17 POPULATION IN THOUSANDS 1925
19	39	— 37	— 31	6	20	57	51	29	9	38	9	1	60	76	70	40	11
23	44	— 8	4	12	..	..	..	..	..	44	..	0	..	52	40	0	9
16	53	— 16	— 16	0	— 45	29	29	45	0	53	8	0	29	37	37	30	16
4	58	— 7	3	10	40	47	37	44	4	58	14	11	41	65	55	30	16
7	59	— 11	47	58	—108	97	—155	47	155	48	1	2	0	70	12	25	23
20	61	— 4	3	7	— 31	27	— 34	6	37	59	53	1	3	65	58	30	20
28	61	— 89	— 88	— 1	19	108	107	45	26	60	15	4	133	150	149	0	8
6	65	—106	— 88	18	45	151	133	45	0	61	16	5	133	171	153	0	8
25	86	— 19	— 74	55	— 4	— 23	— 78	72	76	81	9	17	— 2	67	12	30	44
37	90	— 78	— 58	20	— 1	77	57	14	15	73	59	70	72	168	148	30	93
8	100	— 30	— 30	0	0	— 30	— 30	9	9	30	21		— 21	70	70	0	16
12	105	— 92	— 88	— 4	31	123	119	— 61	30	105	44		149	197	193	30	16
21	120	— 67	—104	37	104	37	0	106	2	119	13	1	2	53	16	30	12
34	120	— 2	67	69	20	22	— 47	90	70	90	0	30	23	122	53	30	317

	1	2	3	4	5	6	7	8	9	10	11	12	13	14	15	16	17
11	148	−64	−14	50	−121	−57	−107	−7	114	148	155	0	7	212	162	30	13
38	151	45	73	28	88	43	15	96	8	134	38	17	23	106	78	30	182
9	163	9	0	0	19	10	10	45	26	163	118		36	154	154	0	20
14	177	−120	−88	32	109	229	197			177			214	297	165	20	18
18	177	89	89	0	114	203	182	125	11	177	52	0	4	266	166	30	43
32	212	109	181	72	181	72	0	185	4	207	22	5	1	103	31	30	22
41	220	−63	75	138	−93	−30	−168	76	169	168	92	52		283	145	30	102
4V	34	−61	3	64	24	85	21	24	0	34	10	0	21	95	31	0	10
1V	43	−92	−88	4	39	131	127	39	0	43	4	0	127	135	131	0	5
7V	58	−94	81	13	17	111	98	33	16	54	21	4	114	152	139	0	6
3V	80	−31	10	41	45	76	35	62	17	80	18	0	52	111	70	0	11
5V	122	−120	−88	32	−53	67	35	31	84	116	85	6	119	242	210	40	8
2V	153	−77	57	20	−22	55	35	71	93	147	76	6	128	230	210	40	10
Cases....	27	27	27	27	26	26	26	25	25	27	25	26	25	27	27	27	27
Range	39 to 153	−120 to 109	−89 to 181	0 to 138	−121 to 181	−97 to 229	−168 to 197	−7 to 185	0 to 169	30 to 207	0 to 155	0 to 70	−21 to 214	37 to 297	12 to 210	.. ..	5 to 317
Median	120.2	−37	3	20.3	20	56	32	45.6	16	80	21.3	1.5	36	122	78	..	16.4

* For explanation of references in this table see Table XVIII.

How To Read Tables XIX and XX: In city number 17, tax collection for the last completed fiscal year began 89 days before the fiscal year began. The school budget was approved by the school board and by the final reviewing authority 200 and 162 days, respectively, before the fiscal year began, so that the latter authority approved the budget 38 days before the former. The assessment roll was completed 213 days before the fiscal year began, 13 days before the budget was adopted by the school board, and 51 days before it was adopted by the final reviewing authority. The tax rate was fixed 151 days before the fiscal year began and 62 days after the assessment roll was completed. The tax warrant was signed 120 days before the beginning of the fiscal year and 31 days after the tax rate was fixed, the last-named event occurring 11 days after the budget was approved by the final authority. The tax warrant was signed 111 days after the budget was adopted by the school board and 73 days after it was approved by the final reviewing authority. A penalty was added to the tax 30 days after collection began. The population in 1925 was, in round numbers, 12,000.

days. This, like the one before, favors Group II, so it cannot be one of the factors sought. Column 12 shows that the span from F to G in the median city favors Group II as does column 9 for the span from D to E. It is evident that the above conclusion holds here also. If these sub-spans are longer in Group I cities than in Group II cities, how can the whole span B to G be shorter in Group I cities? One factor remains to be considered, viz., C to D. Column 7 shows that D occurred 34.8 days before C in the median city of Group I, and thirty-two days after C in the median city of Group II. This permits C to E in the median city of Group I to be short while in the median city of Group II it must be long. Hence the span from B to G does not appear to be significant in explaining the late tax collections in Group II cities. This is substantiated by the span C to G shown in column 15.

Factors Accompanying Delayed Tax Collection.

If the above analysis has been followed carefully, it is apparent that the date when the assessment roll was completed and the date when the budget was reviewed or finally approved are vital factors accompanying delayed tax collection. As further evidence of this, note from column 3, Tables XIX and XX, that the budget was finally adopted seventy-four days before the fiscal year began, C to A, in the median city of Group I, while that event occurred three days after the fiscal year began, A to C, in the median city of Group II. In addition to this the assessment roll was completed thirty-four days before the final adoption of the budget, C to D, in the median city in Group I, but not until thirty-two days after that event in the corresponding city of Group II. Thus the effect of the assessment roll and final adoption of the budget are accumulative in favor of the cities in Group I and unfavorable to those in Group II, enabling the cities of Group I to begin the collection of school taxes nearer the beginning of the fiscal year than was possible in the cities of Group II.

Further Analysis of Groupings.

Having discovered the main factors in the delay of tax collection after the beginning of the fiscal year, their influence in various possible groups of cities was observed. One grouping was made on the basis of the combined collection of school with other local taxes. Such a grouping is given in Table XVII, page 50.

In order to make an analysis of the cities in these groups with respect to tax collection, assessment roll completion, and adoption of the school budget by the reviewing authority, a table was prepared for each group included in Table XVII. Table XXI contains those cities in which school taxes are being collected separate from all other taxes.

How to Interpret Tables XXI to XXVI.

If, for any given city, the figure in column 5 of these Tables is algebraically larger than the corresponding figure in column 4, then D was a more important factor in determining when school taxes could be collected in that city than was C, and vice versa. The size of either of these two figures will be a guide in determining the extent of the influence of the respective factor, and the difference in the size of these two figures will show the relative influence of these two factors. In case these factors do not explain the delay in collecting school taxes after the beginning of the fiscal year, as shown by the figure in column 3, then the figures in either column 7 or 8 and columns 9 and 10 should be of assistance; i.e., if D is the more important factor, see columns 8, 9, and 10; but if C is the more important factor, see columns 7, 9, and 10. As a guide in using these tables the following analyses are given:

Opposite city number 6, in columns 5 and 4, respectively, will be found the numbers 45 and –88. The former number means that the assessment roll was completed in that city 45 days after the fiscal year began. The latter number shows that the budget was approved by the final reviewing authority 88 days before the fiscal year began. According to the empirical rule set up, the date when the assessment roll was completed is the more important factor, since 44 is larger than –88. The difference between these numbers is 132, showing that the date of final adoption of the budget is relatively unimportant in causing a delay in tax collection. This is also evident from the fact that it was adopted 88 days before the year started. Because of the occurrence of these events, school taxes could not have been collected before 45 days after the year began. Column 3 shows they were collected 65 days thereafter. An examination of columns 8, 9, and 10 reveals the remaining 20 days (0 + 16 + 4).

In the case of city No. 16, column 5 shows 45 days elapsing from A to D, but column 4 shows that 16 days passed after the fiscal

TABLE XXI[1]

THE DAY SPAN IS HERE SHOWN BETWEEN CERTAIN EVENTS IN THE SCHOOL TAX CALENDAR OF SEVENTEEN CITIES AND FIVE VILLAGES IN WHICH SCHOOL TAXES ARE COLLECTED SEPARATE FROM ALL OTHER TAXES

	1	2	3	4	5	6	7	8	9	10	11	12
Number of City or Village in Table XVIII	A +	Type of External Income Control*	Days from A to G (a)+	Days from A to C (a)+	Days from A to D (a)+	Days from C to D (a)+	Days from C to E (a)+	Days from D to E +	Days from E to F +	Days from F to G +	Days from A to J (a)+	Tax Payments (b)
3	Aug. 1	I*	31	−74	−61	13	41	4	14	73	−78	
4	Aug. 1	S	58	3	40	37	133	0	16	0	3	
6	Aug. 1	S	65	−88	45	133	−21	9	21	4	−88	
8	Aug. 1	I*	100	30	−121	−30	7	114	155	70	−78	
11	Jan. 1	I**	148	−14	31	−107	149	30	44	0	−88	
12	Aug. 1	S	105	−88	−194	119	−35	6	49	170	−153	
15	Aug. 1	I**	31	−153	45	−41	29	8	8	0		
16	Aug. 1	I*	53	16	114	29	214	0	52	1	−31	
18	Aug. 1	I**	177	−89	20	182	60	11	9	2	−88	
19	Aug. 1	S	39	−31	−31	51	3	9	53	115	−214	
20	Aug. 1	I*	61	3	−190	34	7	37	50	0	3	
22	Jan. 1	S	0	−172		−18		25				
23	Aug. 1	I*	−44	4	−153	−17	−8	9	41	42	−122	
26	Aug. 1	S	−61	−136	19	107	133	26	15	1	−88	
28	Aug. 1	S	61	−88	−122	−34	0	34	88	0	−88	
29	Aug. 1	I**	0	−88	−286	−269	5	274	21	22	−17	
31	Aug. 1		31	17								
1V	Aug. 1	S	43	−88	39	127	127	0	4	0	−88	
3V	Aug. 1	S	80	10	45	35	52	17	18	0	10	
4V	Aug. 1	S	34	3	24	21	21	0	10	11	3	
6V	Aug. 1	S	31	−88	−407	−319	10	329	98	4	−88	
7V	Aug. 1	S	58	−81	17	98	114	16	21		−88	

[1] Explanation for Tables XXI–XXVI inclusive.

* Types of External Income Control.

    D Dependent school system.

    I* School budget either is not submitted for review or the reviewing authority has no power to change it.

    I** School budget may be reduced by the reviewing authority but the school board may reinstate the original amount by a three-fourths vote.

    S School budget is approved by the legal voters.

+ Events in school tax calendar.

    A. Date when the school fiscal year began.

    B. Date when the budget was adopted by the school board.

    C. Date when the budget was adopted by the final reviewing authority.

    D. Date when the assessment-roll was completed.

    E. Date when the tax rate was fixed.

    F. Date when the tax warrant was signed.

    G. Date tax collection began.

    J. Date annual estimate is required to be submitted for review.

(*) A minus sign in front of a number indicates that the second of the two events symbolized by the letters at the head of the column took place before the first event.

(b) An x in this column after any city indicates that school taxes therein are payable in two installments.

How To Read Table XXI: In city No. 8, whose last completed school fiscal year began Aug. 1, 1925, the school system is absolutely independent. The collection of the school tax for the above fiscal year began 100 days after Aug. 1, 1925; the budget was adopted by the final reviewing authority 30 days after Aug. 1, the assessment-roll was completed 0 days after Aug. 1, and 30 days before the budget was adopted by the final reviewing authority: the school tax rate was fixed 21 days before the budget was adopted by the final reviewing authority and 9 days after the assessment-roll was completed; the tax warrant authorizing the collection of the school tax was signed 21 days after the tax rate was fixed and tax collection began 70 days after the tax warrant was signed.

TABLE XXII(¹)

The Day Span is Here Shown Between Certain Events in the School Tax Calendar in Eight Cities in Which School Taxes Are Collected at the Same Time as City Taxes

Number of City or Village in Table XVIII	1 A +	2 Type of External Income Control*	3 Days from A to G +(a)	4 Days from A to C +(a)	5 Days from A to D +(a)	6 Days from C to D +(a)	7 Days from C to E +	8 Days from D to E +	9 Days from E to F +	10 Days from F to G +	11 Days from A to J +(a)	12 Tax Payments (b)
2	Aug. 1	I*	23	-116	0	116	117	1	17	5	-198	
27	Aug. 1	S	31	3	- 12	- 15	1	16	26	1	3	
32	Jan. 1	I*	212	181	181	0	4	4	22	5	120	
34	Jan. 1	D	120	67	20	- 47	23	70	0	30	1	
37	Jan. 1	D	90	- 58	- 1	57	72	15	59	17	61	
38	Jan. 1	D	151	73	88	15	23	8	38	17	61	
39	Aug. 1	I*	- 31	- 89	- 69	20	21	1	31	6	181	
41	Jan. 1	I*	220	75	93	-168	1	169	92	52	61	

(¹) Explanation of this table is the same as that of Table XXI, p. 64.

TABLE XXIII(1)

THE DAY SPAN IS HERE SHOWN BETWEEN CERTAIN EVENTS IN THE SCHOOL TAX CALENDAR IN FOUR CITIES AND TWO VILLAGES IN WHICH SCHOOL TAXES ARE COLLECTED WITH STATE AND COUNTY TAXES

NUMBER OF CITY OR VILLAGE IN TABLE XVIII	1 A +	2 TYPE OF EXTERNAL INCOME CONTROL*	3 DAYS FROM A to G +(a)	4 DAYS FROM A to C +(a)	5 DAYS FROM A to D +(a)	6 DAYS FROM C to D +(a)	7 DAYS FROM C to E +	8 DAYS FROM D to E +	9 DAYS FROM E to F +	10 DAYS FROM F to G +	11 DAYS FROM A to J +(a)	12 TAX PAYMENTS (b)
9	Aug. 1	I*	163	9	19	10	36	26	118	0	··	
10	Jan. 1	D	1	− 58	− 92	− 34	41	75	16	2	− 92	
14	Aug. 1	S	177	− 88	109	197	··	··	··	··	− 88	
21	Jan. 1	I*	120	104	104	0	2	2	13	1	− 73	
2V	July 1	S	153	− 57	− 22	35	128	93	76	6	− 57	x
5V	Aug. 1	S	122	− 88	− 53	35	119	84	85	6	− 88	x

(1) Explanation of this table is the same as that of Table XXXI, p. 64.

year began before the school budget was approved by the reviewing authority. This situation is somewhat different from that shown in the other analysis. As before, it is evident that the completion of the assessment roll is the more important factor, but since the measures are nearly the same size, it is not the only factor affecting the late collection of taxes. Sixteen of the 53 days (column 3) are accounted for by the delayed approval of the budget, while 29 days (column 6) are due to the completion of the assessment roll after the budget had been adopted. As before, reference to columns 7, 9, and 10 reveals the remaining 8 days (0 + 8 + 0). These two cases were chosen because the figures in column 5 were the same for both cities, and to illustrate the futility of depending upon any one figure to tell the story.

Tables XXII, XXIII, XXIV, XXV, and XXVI can be interpreted as explained above. They are exactly the same figures for the various cities, but the criteria used for grouping them were different.

Analysis of Groupings Continued.

It should be noted that all the cities and villages in Table XXI have either special or fiscally independent school systems. This probably accounts in some measure for the fact that they all collect their school taxes separately. An examination of column 3 of this table shows that the cities and villages in this group compare rather favorably with the entire group of fifty cities and villages with respect to late tax collection, even though only seven of the twenty-two were in Group I, shown in Table XIX, page 58. There are only two rather extreme cases in the group, however.

An analysis of the situations in the individual cities, following the method shown above, shows that in most of the cities and villages completion of the assessment roll was a determining factor whenever taxes were collected more than thirty-one days after the fiscal year began. In six cities there was considerable delay in fixing the tax rate after the assessed valuation and amount of the budget were known, and in a like number of cities fifty or more days elapsed while the tax-rolls were being extended. Five cities delayed collection of taxes for more than forty days after the warrant had been signed for their collection. The contrast of these cities with the fifteen in which four or less days so elapsed is significant.

TABLE XXIV(¹)

THE DAY SPAN IS HERE SHOWN BETWEEN CERTAIN EVENTS IN THE SCHOOL TAX CALENDAR OF FOURTEEN CITIES IN WHICH SCHOOL TAXES ARE COLLECTED WITH STATE, COUNTY, AND CITY TAXES

Number of City in Table XVIII	A (+)	Type of External Income Control*	Days from A to G +(a)	Days from A to C +(a)	Days from A to D +(a)	Days from C to D +(a)	Days from C to E +(a)	Days from D to E +	Days from E to F +	Days from F to G +	Days from A to J +(a)	Tax Payments (b)
1	Jan. 1	D	0	−25	−43	−18	−1	19	21	3	−61	x
5	Jan. 1	I*	31	−12	−93	−81	−81	0	122	2	−92	x
7	Jan. 1	I*	59	−47	−108	−155		155	1	11	−31	x
13	Jan. 1	I**	−31	−80	−113	−33	0	40	27	15	−122	x
17	May 1	I*	−89	−162	−213	−51	7	62	31	31	−233	x
24	Jan. 1	I**	0	−38	−133	−95	11	96	33	4	−92	x
25	Jan. 1	I*	86	−74	−4	−78	1	76	9	5	−24	x
30	Jan. 1	D	17	−86	−103	−17		86	29	5	−83	x
33	Jan. 1	I**	14	−62	−114	−52	2	67	61	0	−92	x
35	Jan. 1	I*	0	−74	−79	−5	69	11	67	1	−122	x
36	Jan. 1	D	11	−63	−124	−61	15	72	51	12	−92	x
40	Jan. 1	I**	0	−14	−129	−115	6	115	0	14	−61	x
42	Jan. 1	I**	8	−14	−91	−77	11	88	10	1	−61	x
43	Jan. 1	I**	1	−73	−122	−49	0	49	42	32	−139	x

(¹) Explanation of this table is the same as that of Table XXI, p. 64.

In the cities in which school taxes and city taxes are collected together—but separate from other taxes—as shown in Table XXII,
situations analogous to the findings in Table XXI are apparent.
This group contains three cities having dependent school systems,
in all of which taxes were collected at least three months after the
fiscal year began. However, in two cities having independent
school systems, tax collection was delayed longer than in any of
the three dependent systems. Three of the cities in this group
were in Group I, Table XIX.

Table XXIII contains the four cities and two villages in which
school taxes were collected at the same time as those for state
and county. This combination is bad from the school standpoint,
for tax collection is delayed until county taxes are levied and
collected. In only one city, Elmira, were taxes collected earlier
than one hundred and twenty days after the fiscal year began.
As a group this one ranks below both of the preceding.

Table XXIV shows the fourteen cities in which school taxes
are being collected at the same time as state, county, and city
taxes. This group is outstanding in several respects. Only two
cities in this group began to collect their taxes more than thirty-
one days after the fiscal year began, which date, in every case but
one, was January 1. The school budget received final approval
before the fiscal year began in every city but two. In every city
the assessed valuation for the following tax year was known before
the school budget received final approval, and in advance of the
beginning of the fiscal year. In still another respect this group is
unique. In all but one of these cities taxes are payable in two
installments. In only two cities, New Rochelle and Poughkeepsie,
is there a fee added for this privilege. Excessive lapses of time
can be noted between some events in the tax calendar, but, as
noted, these are not peculiar to this group of cities. These cities
have taken the necessary steps properly to coördinate the financial
calendar with the opening of the fiscal year. Other cities of the
state are now reorganizing their financial calendar looking to a
solution of the problem which has been solved by the above cities.

It is surprising to find that in the cities in which school taxes
are collected with all other taxes a better coördination with the
fiscal year has resulted than in those cities in which school taxes
are collected separately. Perhaps this superior coördination is the
result of having the school fiscal year coincide with the city fiscal

TABLE XXV(1)

The Day Span is Here Shown Between Certain Events in the School Tax Calendar of Twenty Cities and Six Villages Whose School Fiscal Year Begins Aug. 1

	1	2	3	4	5	6	7	8	9	10	11	12
Number of City or Village in Table XVIII	A +	Type of External Income Control*	Days from A to G +(a)	Days from A to C +(a)	Days from A to D +(a)	Days from C to D +(a)	Days from C to E +(a)	Days from D to E +	Days from E to F +	Days from F to G +	Days from A to J +(a)	Tax Payments (b)
2	Aug. 1	I*	23	−116	0	116	117	1	17	5	−198	
3	Aug. 1	I*	31	−74	−61	13				73	−78	
4	Aug. 1	S	58	−3	40	37	41	4	14	0	−3	
6	Aug. 1	S	65	−88	45	133	133	9	16	4	−88	
8	Aug. 1	I*	100	−30	0	−30	−21	9	21	70		
9	Aug. 1	S	163	−9	19	10	36	26	118	0		
12	Aug. 1	S	105	−88	31	119	149	30	44		−88	
14	Aug. 1	I**	177	−88	109	197				170	−88	
15	Aug. 1	I*	31	−153	−194	−41	−35	6	49	0	−153	
16	Aug. 1	I*	53	16	45	29	29	0	8	0		
18	Aug. 1	I**	177	−89	114	182	214	11	52	1		
19	Aug. 1	S	39	−31	20	51	60	9	9	2	−31	
20	Aug. 1	S	61	1	−31	−34	3	37	53	42	−88	
23	Aug. 1	I*	44	4	−153	−17				1	−3	
26	Aug. 1	I*	−61	−136	12	−15	−8	9	41	1	−122	
27	Aug. 1	S	31	−3	19	−107	1	16	26	0		
28	Aug. 1	S	61	−88	−122	−34	133	26	15	22	−88	
29	Aug. 1	S	0	−88	−286	−269	0	34	88	6	−88	
31	Aug. 1	I**	31	−17	69	20	5	274	21		−17	
39	Aug. 1	I*	−31	−89			21	1	31		−181	
1V	Aug. 1	S	43	−88	39	127	127	0	4	0	−88	
3V	Aug. 1	S	80	10	45	35	52	17	18	0	−10	
4V	Aug. 1	S	34	−3	24	21	21	0	10	0	−3	
5V	Aug. 1	S	122	−88	−53	−35	119	84	85	6	−88	
6V	Aug. 1	S	31	−88	−407	−319	10	329	98	11	−88	
7V	Aug. 1	S	58	−81	17	98	114	16	21	4	−88	

(1) Explanation of this table is the same as that of Table XXXI, p. 64.

year. To test this possibility, the cities and villages studied were grouped on that basis and an analysis made.

An inspection of Table XXV discloses the fact that in only nine, or 34.6 per cent, of the cities and villages whose school fiscal year begins August 1, are school taxes collected as early as thirty-one days after the beginning of the year. Within the period from thirty-one days to sixty-one days after August 1, nine more cities or villages collected school taxes, so that twelve, or 69.2 per cent, of the cities or villages probably began to receive tax money within sixty-one days after the fiscal year began. It is as justifiable for school systems, whose fiscal year begins August 1, to begin the collection of taxes sixty-one days after that date, as for school systems, whose fiscal year begins January 1, to begin to collect taxes thirty-one days after that date, for in the former systems there is but small need for money during August, while in the latter systems school expenditures are being made from the beginning of the fiscal year.

Table XXVI, containing the cities whose school fiscal years began January 1, shows that of these twenty-two cities, thirteen, or 59.1 per cent, began the collection of school taxes within thirty-one days after that date. This is a better showing than that made by the cities and villages whose fiscal year began August 1, when the same delay after the fiscal year is considered. A fairer comparison would result, however,' if the latter group of cities were given the advantage of a two-months' delay, which, as shown above, is financially comparable with a one-month delay in the former group. When such a comparison is made, 59.1 per cent with 69.2 per cent, it is evident that whatever advantage might be claimed would favor the group whose fiscal year began August 1. Be that as it may, the fact remains that there is a great opportunity for improvement along the line of the discussion of this chapter, and the findings herein recorded should furnish the basis for constructive reorganization in the financial calendars of the many cities and villages wherein the need for the same is apparent from this study. Doubtless some of the cities not covered in this study need the same type of reorganization in order to provide a more economical financial program. It is hoped that these findings will be of value to such cities.

TABLE XXVI(¹)

The Day Span is Here Shown Between Certain Events in the School Tax Calendar of Twenty-three Cities Whose School Fiscal Year Begins Jan. 1

Number of City or Village in Table XVIII	1 A +	2 Type of External Income Control*	3 Days from A to G +(a)	4 Days from A to C +(a)	5 Days from A to D +(a)	6 Days from C to D +(a)	7 Days from C to E +(a)	8 Days from D to E +	9 Days from E to F +	10 Days from F to G +	11 Days from A to J +(a)	12 Tax Payments (b)
1	Jan. 1	D	0	− 25	− 43	− 18	1	19	21	3	− 61	
5	Jan. 1	I*	31	− 12	− 93	− 81	− 81	0	122	2	− 92	
7	Jan. 1	I*	59	− 47	− 108	− 155	0	155	1	11	− 31	
10	Jan. 1	D	1	− 58	− 92	− 34	41	75	16	2	− 92	
11	Jan. 1	I***	− 31	− 14	− 121	− 107	7	114	155	0	− 78	
13	Jan. 1	I***	120	− 80	− 113	− 33	7	40	27	15	− 122	
21	Jan. 1	I*	0	− 104	− 104	0	2	2	13	1	73	
22	Jan. 1	I***	86	− 172	− 190	− 18	7	25	50	115	− 214	
24	Jan. 1	I***	17	− 38	− 133	− 95	1	96	33	4	− 92	
25	Jan. 1	I*	212	− 74	− 4	− 78	− 2	76	9	5	24	
30	Jan. 1	I*	14	− 86	− 103	− 17	69	86	29	5	− 83	
32	Jan. 1	D	120	− 181	− 181	0	4	4	22	5	120	
33	Jan. 1	D	0	− 62	− 114	− 52	15	67	61	0	− 92	
34	Jan. 1	I***	11	− 67	− 20	− 47	23	70	0	30	1	
35	Jan. 1	I*	90	− 74	− 79	− 5	6	11	67	1	− 122	
36	Jan. 1	D	151	− 63	− 124	− 61	11	72	51	12	− 92	
37	Jan. 1	D	0	− 58	− 1	− 57	72	15	59	17	− 61	
38	Jan. 1	D	220	− 73	− 88	− 15	23	8	38	17	− 61	
40	Jan. 1	I*	8	− 14	− 129	− 115	0	115	0	14	− 61	
41	Jan. 1	I***	1	− 75	− 93	− 168	1	169	92	52	− 61	
42	Jan. 1	I***		− 14	− 91	− 77	11	88	10	1	− 61	
43	Jan. 1	I***		− 73	− 122	− 49	0	49	42	32	− 139	

(¹) Explanation of this table is the same as that of Table XXI, p. 64.

The Fiscal Year and the Submission of the Annual School Estimate

At the close of Chapter II it was stated that further consideration would be given to the proper date for the submission of the annual school estimate for review. Accepting the judgment of authorities in this field relative to the desirability of collecting taxes early in the fiscal year, and having discovered a group of cities in which this ideal is almost universally being realized, the time for such a consideration seems propitious.

Technique Used

When determining the proper relationship which should exist between the date for submission of the annual estimate and the fiscal year, two criteria must be satisfied: (1) the date for submitting the annual estimate must be far enough in advance of the beginning of the fiscal year to permit the occurrence of those events which in the scheme of operation should transpire before that fiscal year begins; and (2) it must be near enough to the beginning of the fiscal year to permit a sound basis for arriving at that estimate.

The date upon which the school budget estimate should be submitted for review can not be arbitrarily chosen if these criteria are to govern. Nor can present practice be accepted without critical evaluation.

This problem, as it pertains to the municipal budget, has been considered by authorities in the field of municipal finance. While their findings may not furnish the solution of the present problem of the school budget estimate, they might materially assist in its solution. If their findings were tested out to determine their practicability in the school situation, a solution of the present problem might be found. Believing that such a technique would be fruitful, it was followed by the author. The results of applying this technique follow.

Application of Technique

Criteria Set Up by Authorities in Municipal Finance. In setting up a standard budget section for city charters, the Governmental Research Conference Committee [14] specified that the annual

[14] Buck, A. E. *Budget Making*, Appendix IV, p. 219. D. Appleton and Company. 1921.

budget be submitted to the council not later than six weeks before the end of the year, and that the appropriation ordinance based on the budget submitted be passed by the council not later than the beginning of the fiscal year.

In a survey of Newark, N. J., the Bureau of Municipal Research recommended a budget calendar as follows: [15]

Nov. 1. Submission of division and bureau head's estimates to the commissioner at the head of the department.

Nov. 1–10. Consolidation and revision of such estimates.

By Nov. 10. Submit to commission as a whole and to the auditor for comparison and consolidation.

By Dec. 20. Public hearing.

By Dec. 31. Final adoption.

It should be noted that the former authority provides forty-two days and the latter authority fifty-one days preceding the beginning of the fiscal year for all details incident to the adoption of the budget by the common council after it has been submitted to them. It should also be noted that no time is provided between the adoption of the budget and the beginning of the fiscal year for the necessary duties which must be performed before taxes can be collected. This means that tax collection cannot begin with the fiscal year if these recommendations are followed.

Findings in Cities In Which School and City Taxes Are Collected at the Same Time. Up to this point nothing has been said about column 11, Tables XXII and XXIV, pages 66 and 69, respectively. This column contains data for the present analysis. Column 11, Table XXIV, shows that in three cities the annual school estimate is to be submitted for review two hundred and thirty-three and one hundred and twenty-two days, respectively, before the fiscal year begins. These annual estimates were not adopted by the school board until thirty-three, thirty-six, and thirty-four days, respectively, after the date set for such submission,[16] and yet tax collection was begun eighty-nine, thirty-one, and zero days, respectively, before the fiscal year began.[17] In the city in which this estimate is required one hundred and thirty-nine days in advance of the fiscal year, the reviewing authorities took a much longer time in performing that duty than in most of the other cities. An analysis of column 11, Table XXII, shows similar

[15] *A Survey of the Government, Finance, and Administration of the City of Newark, N. J.* Bureau of Municipal Research. New York. Nov., 1919, Part I.

[16] See Column 3, Tables IV and VI, pp. 17 and 19.

[17] See Column 7, Table XVIII, pp. 52 and 53.

negligence on the part of reviewing authorities and delay in assessment roll completion in these cities which require the estimate to be submitted one hundred and eighty-one and one hundred and ninety-eight days, respectively, ahead of the fiscal year. It is evident, therefore, that in these cities the estimate is required to be submitted for review earlier than is necessary in order to insure tax collection soon after the beginning of the fiscal year.

An analysis of the occurrence of events in the four cities of Table XXIV, requiring the submission of this estimate ninety-two days in advance of the fiscal year, reveals the fact that this day span is long enough to satisfy the first criterion. Whether or not it is too long depends upon local conditions. A similar analysis in the three cities requiring this estimate sixty-one days prior to the beginning of the fiscal year culminates in the same conclusion. This conclusion is further supported by an inspection of Table XXII, page 66, in which three other cities require the submission of the school estimate sixty-one days prior to the beginning of the fiscal year. While tax collection in all of these cities did not actually begin soon after the beginning of the fiscal year, evidences of the reasons for these delays are apparent.

In the cities of these two tables whose school estimate was submitted later than sixty-one days before the fiscal year began, no evidence was found which would warrant the conclusion that fewer than sixty-one days were needed in which to review the budget and prepare for tax collection near the opening of the fiscal year.

In these cities the school budget becomes a part of the city budget and the school estimate is usually presented at the same time as other departmental estimates. This is unfortunate from the school standpoint, for the preparation of the school estimate then comes at a time when the school officials are extremely busy with the proper beginning of a new school term. It also means that this estimate must be prepared earlier than would be necessary if it were not considered along with other departmental estimates.

Authorities in educational administration are opposed to the present consideration of the school budget by municipal authorities and are convinced that the present degree of dependence of school systems on the municipal government in New York cities is harmful to the cause of education. It is most interesting to note in this connection that in one of the absolutely dependent school systems of the state the above viewpoint has been accepted by the framers of the city charter. That charter provides that all departmental estimates, except that of the department of public instruction, are to be submitted on November 1, while the estimate of the public instruction department is not to be submitted until December 31.[18]

Conclusions

This analysis reveals the fact that in most cities in which the school tax is collected at the same time as the city tax, the collection of school taxes could begin soon after the beginning of the fiscal year if the budget estimate had been submitted for review only sixty days before the school fiscal year began. In all other cities its submission ninety days in advance of the fiscal year would provide ample time for its consideration. It is therefore concluded, that in no case should the school estimate be submitted for review earlier than ninety days ahead of the fiscal year and that a period of sixty days is sufficient in which to consider this estimate and prepare for the collection of taxes early in the fiscal year. These day spans are longer than those previously shown to be recommended by authorities in municipal finance, but it will be recalled that they did not provide for preparation for tax collection early in the fiscal year.

As was pointed out earlier in this study, it is highly desirable and necessary that the assessment roll be completed, if possible, before the school budget is adopted by the school board and certainly before it is approved by the final reviewing authority. No adequate program can be adopted so long as the assessment roll is left to chance for completion. Local conditions, however, will govern the distribution of time intervals between the submission of the annual estimate and the date when tax collection will begin. A carefully considered program following the recommendations set forth above is sure to bring good results.

Findings in Cities in Which School and City Taxes Are Collected Separately. Those cities and villages included in this study, in which school taxes are collected at a different time than are the general city taxes, were considered earlier in this chapter.[19] At

---

[18] *Rochester City Charter*, Sec. 28, according to a report of a study of the financial condition and practices of the city of Rochester, New York, by the Rochester Bureau of Municipal Research, Dec., 1923.

[19] See Tables XXI and XXIII, pp. 64 and 67.

that time, however, no especial attention was given to the submission of the annual school estimate in those cities. Since the adoption of the school budget therein is not dependent upon the adoption of the city budget, one might expect that the annual school estimate would be submitted for review only a short time before the fiscal year began and that tax collection would begin soon after the beginning of the fiscal year. This would be the situation if the tax calendar were properly coördinated with the fiscal year. It has already been shown, however, that tax collection took place some time after the year started in most of those cities and villages.

To discover the situation with respect to the requirement for the submission of the annual estimate, column 11, Tables XXI and XXIII, pages 64 and 67, should be consulted. Here, as in the case of the other group of cities discussed above, there is evidence that in some cities this estimate is required much earlier than is necessary. To require that this estimate be presented one hundred and twenty-two, one hundred and fifty-three, and two hundred and fourteen days, respectively, before the year begins is contrary to sound principles of budgetary procedure. In ten of these cities and villages this estimate must be submitted eighty-eight days before August 1. This period is determined by the school law which sets the first Tuesday in May as the date for the annual school meeting at which time the budget for the succeeding fiscal year is to be adopted. This date is an unfortunate one for many reasons. No attempt will be made to present an exhaustive analysis of these reasons, but in light of the findings of this study a few reasons are given in the next paragraph.

The first Tuesday in May finds the school executive overburdened with duties incident to the closing of a school year; the report made at that time is necessarily incomplete and difficult to prepare; an accurate basis for determining state moneys to be received the following year is not yet available; the state tax equalization report has not been received and hence an estimate for state moneys from the equalization fund cannot be accurately made; the type of review in these cities makes unnecessary the adoption of the budget at this early date so that neither of the criteria stated above is satisfied by such a submission date. These are a few of the outstanding objections to this date for the annual school meeting.

A few cities have been allowed to change the date of the annual meeting and are now holding it on either the first or second Tuesday in August. These dates overcome the objections set forth above, but, unless provision is made so that an official assessment roll may be prepared, considerable delay in the collection of the school tax will result. If the assessment roll is ready at such a meeting in late July or early August, the tax roll can be made up and collection begun before large expenditures must be made. School tax collection near the middle of the calendar year in these cities and the collection of the city tax early in the calendar year would provide a good substitute for the two installment collections found in the cities in which school, state, county, and city taxes are being collected together. In six cities (Batavia, Canandaigua, Geneva, Hornell, Mechanicville and Olean), and four of the villages (Green Island, Herkimer, Ilion and Seneca Falls) the school officials designate the date upon which the school taxes are to be collected. With active coöperation between these officials and city officials an equitable arrangement could be made to the mutual advantage of the city, the school, and the taxpayers.

SUMMARY

In this chapter the viewpoint of legislators and authorities on municipal finance has been shown relative to the harmony which should exist between the dates of the financial calendar and the fiscal year. These authorities apparently agree upon the advisability of having the budget for the succeeding year adopted before the close of the current fiscal year. Tax collection should be begun early in the fiscal year in order that interest on temporary loans need not be added to the already overburdened taxpayer.

The relationship existing between the events in the tax calendar and the beginning of the fiscal year in the city school districts of the various states is not apparent from studies or publications at hand, and many departments of education informed the author that such information on the cities of their states was not available. In some states these dates are uniform throughout the cities of the state, and in others the school district does not need to depend upon local taxation for the support of schools.

From an analysis of the data gathered in the present study, it was discovered that school taxes are being levied in the main by the common councils of the cities in the State of New York. In eleven of the forty-three cities studied this tax is being levied by the school board, and in three cities by the board of supervisors. In all but four of these cities the school tax is being collected by a municipal officer. The village school districts usually employ a tax collector who is not associated with the village government. In the counties of Westchester and Nassau, school taxes are collected by the receiver of taxes for the town in which the village is located.

In seventeen cities and five villages studied, school taxes are collected when no other taxes are being paid; in eight cities school taxes are collected at the same time as city taxes; in four cities and two villages they are collected at the same time as state and county taxes; and in fourteen cities they are collected at the same time as state, county, and city taxes. All of the cities except Albany in the last group mentioned provide that these taxes may be paid in two installments. This is the only group in which this privilege is extended, except that in Nassau County, in which Hempstead and Lynbrook are located, state, county, and school taxes may be paid in two installments. A comparison made of the extent to which school taxes were being collected at the same time as other local taxes in 1917 with the present method of collection failed to show any distinct trend in the changes which have taken place. Three of the eight cities making a change in this respect are now collecting school taxes separately from all others, whereas, before, they were combining these with some other tax.

It was shown that school taxes were collected from eighty-nine days before to two hundred and twenty days after the beginning of the fiscal year in the various cities studied. It was also found that the date when the assessment roll was completed and the date of the final adoption of the school budget by the reviewing authority were the two most influential factors in the lack of coördination of tax collection with the beginning of the fiscal year. The length of time which elapsed between the adoption of the budget by the school board and the tax collection date was found to be neither a function of the size of the city nor of the number of days tax collection was delayed after the beginning of the fiscal year.

Having discovered the main factors preventing the early collection of school taxes, the cities were divided into four groups according to the type of tax collection therein. A study of these groups in the light of previous findings showed that the group in which school, state, county, and city taxes are all being collected at the same time had most satisfactorily coördinated the tax calendar and the fiscal year. Only two cities in this group failed to collect taxes as early as thirty-one days after the fiscal year began.

Since in all but one of the cities in the above group the school fiscal year began January 1, the cities were again divided on the basis of the date when the fiscal year began to see if that fact was the one favoring that group of cities. However, an analysis of these groups failed to confirm that tentative conclusion.

After a careful study of the data at hand, it was concluded that the annual school estimate should not be submitted earlier than ninety days prior to the beginning of the fiscal year. This will be a longer period than necessary in many cities and should not be accepted as ideal, for it was also found that the submission of this estimate sixty days prior to the beginning of the fiscal year was practical and provided ample time in which the other events of the tax calendar could take place. The nearer the annual estimate is to the beginning of the fiscal year the better, provided sufficient time remains in which may be accomplished the many details incident to the collection of taxes soon after the fiscal year begins.

The cities in which school taxes are being collected separately from the general city taxes have not taken advantage of the possibilities which such collection provides. In a majority of these cities the annual school estimate must be submitted eighty-eight or more days before the fiscal year begins. This is much earlier than is necessary under the type of external control exercised over these school systems. The present date for the annual school meeting and submission of the school budget for adoption, although prescribed by school law, is not a very satisfactory one. If the annual meeting were held late in July or early in August with provision made whereby an assessment roll would be ready for extension at that time, the school tax could be collected soon thereafter in time to meet school needs.

CHAPTER V

ADMINISTRATIVE CONTROL OF INCOME

INTRODUCTION

The preceding chapter has shown the extent to which the collection of school taxes is delayed after the beginning of the fiscal year, together with the factors which are influential in bringing about that delay. Inasmuch as the need for money is apparent either at once or soon after the beginning of the fiscal year, the question of how these needs are met when tax money is not forthcoming immediately arises. The first part of this chapter will be concerned with an answer to that query.

After tax collection gets under way, the money therefrom is often received faster than it is needed, even though it may have been needed before its collection began. During the early weeks of this collection, enough money to support the schools for the full year or for at least a half year is due and payable. This surplus money is then held in the treasury until future needs require its expenditure. The safe and economical administration of this surplus is an important phase of income control. The latter part of this chapter will be devoted to a consideration of such administration in the cities and villages studied.

ADMINISTRATIVE ADJUSTMENTS PRECEDING THE RECEIPT OF TAX MONEYS

Need for Adjustments

In all the cities included in this study the school systems operate in accordance with an annual budget which is usually adopted by the school board before the fiscal year begins.[1] The expenditures provided therein are supposed to represent the needs during the fiscal year for which the budget is prepared. Receipts from various sources are provided with which to meet these needs. In

[1] See column 2, Table XVIII, pp. 52 and 53.

theory the actual needs and the actual receipts should be equal so that at the end of the fiscal year all bills will have been met and the treasury will have been depleted. When this ideal has been attained, expenditures cannot be made in the new fiscal year until receipts for that year's needs have arrived. Most school systems depend upon local taxes for these receipts so that tax collection at the beginning of the year becomes desirable. However, it has been shown that tax collection rarely begins on the first day of the fiscal year in the cities and villages studied. Since the needs arise almost at once after the fiscal year has begun, and since the school tax is not being collected at once in these cities, some administrative adjustments must have been made therein.

Adjustments Encountered

Accordingly, an effort was made to discover what was being done to meet these needs preceding the receipt of tax moneys. It was found that four adjustments were being made in one or more of the cities included in this study. These adjustments, stated in the order of greatest frequency encountered, are: (1) the advancement of money from the general city fund with which to meet school needs; (2) negotiation for short-term loans by the school board in anticipation of taxes; (3) surplus revenue from the previous year with which to meet school needs previous to the collection of taxes; and (4) delaying the payment of bills until tax moneys are received. Some idea of the extent to which each of these adjustments was encountered will now be given.

Frequency of Occurrence of Adjustments

In twenty-five of the forty-three cities visited, the problem of late collection of school taxes is a municipal problem as well as a problem for the school officials to solve. In these twenty-five cities money is made available out of the general city funds for school expenditures during the fiscal year. Very often the city budget of which the school budget is a part has not been approved, nor has the appropriation ordinance specifying the amount which can be expended for school purposes been passed, until many weeks after the beginning of the fiscal year. However, school expenses continue and are paid by the city treasurer. In one city these expenditures continue over a period of six months before the budget is passed, so that the superintendent in reality budgets only for four school months during the year, September to December, inclusive. The inadequacy of such procedure is obvious.

Needless to say, these cities are dependent upon local taxes for current moneys. When tax collection does not begin until after the fiscal year has begun, money is often not available with which to meet school and city needs early in the fiscal year. The city officials must then borrow money with which to meet these needs. The interest on these loans is usually paid out of the general city fund so that the school systems therein are not directly affected by the lack of city funds. However, the interest on this money must be paid by the taxpayers of the locality, thereby increasing the burden of taxation. This will have an effect upon the amount which the people are willing to raise for the schools. Proper coördination of the tax calendar with the fiscal year will save this added expense to the people upon whom the burden of taxation rests. Because late collection of taxes does not affect the school budget directly, schoolmen in these cities are prone to regard the problem as of no consequence to them. They should, however, grasp the problem in its entirety and assist in its solution in their localities.

The second adjustment made for the purpose of supplying funds with which to meet school needs at the beginning of the fiscal year before taxes are collected is the negotiation for short-term loans, by the school board, in anticipation of the receipt of taxes. This method, as pointed out above, was being employed in some of the cities following the first method of adjustment. In those cities, however, this adjustment was made by the city authorities and not by the school authorities as in the school systems now under consideration. In eight cities and four villages the school board had to borrow money in anticipation of taxes, due to the late collection of school taxes. These loans ranged in amount from $5,000 to $1,750,000, and were outstanding from a few days to several months. While the interest payments on these loans were but a small fraction of total annual expenditures, the fact remains that those amounts could have been saved to the systems if taxes had been collected early enough in the fiscal year to have made borrowing in anticipation thereof unnecessary.

The third adjustment which was found in a few cities was the practice of planning for greater receipts than expenditures, so that a considerable cash balance would be on hand at the end of the year. This cash would then be used to meet the school needs in the next fiscal year before tax moneys were received, thus relieving the board of the necessity for borrowing. This method is being followed by seven of the school systems studied. In one of these the balance was not large enough to meet all expenditures before the taxes were received. Short-term loans provided the balance therein.

This method appeals to many as a desirable practice in that it saves the interest which would otherwise be paid on short-term loans. That fact can not be denied, but the loss to the community of the use of this money for other purposes may be many times as great as the momentary saving of interest. To build up such a working balance, it was necessary to levy a larger tax than current needs required, a practice contrary to accepted principles of taxation. After this surplus fund has been increased to workable proportions, it stands as a temptation to future school boards, for it is not controlled by the budget. Authorities in public finance are agreed upon the undesirability of maintaining sinking funds. There are but few evils of sinking fund administration which are not at the same time potential evils in the administration of surplus revenue funds. When it is recalled that the condition which has occasioned the building up of these questionable reserve funds can be entirely removed by the simple device of properly adjusting tax collection dates to current needs, one can not see any justification for their continuance.

The fourth adjustment found in a very few cities was that of delaying the payment of bills until tax moneys were received. If goods were bought for delivery during the period previous to the collection of taxes, these goods were billed for a date subsequent to such collection. This method appears to be advantageous to the school system. It is a makeshift, however, and if practiced extensively would not only give the school system a low commercial rating, but would affect the prices which must be asked for such goods. This method is used more extensively at the close of the fiscal year after allowances for the then current year have been exhausted. Most of the school systems visited, however, profess to pay commercial invoices promptly.

The Real Adjustment

It is gratifying to note that the necessity for these adjustments is decreasing. Several cities have already taken the necessary steps properly to coördinate tax collection with the beginning of the fiscal- year, and other cities are now in the process of making such changes. This coördination is the real adjustment which should be made by all cities now practicing any of the adjustments enumerated above. Cities which are known to be moving the tax calendar forward so that taxes will be collected nearer the beginning of the fiscal year, include Jamestown, Rochester, Syracuse, and Schenectady. It is hoped that this study will add momentum to this movement, for it is the one adjustment which is economical, practical, and in accord with sound business procedure.

ADMINISTRATION OF SCHOOL MONEYS

Custodian of School Moneys

In thirty-five[2] of the forty-three cities studied, the custodian of municipal moneys is also the custodian of school moneys. In the remaining eight cities and in the seven villages there is a school treasurer, or a bank which acts in that capacity, having no official connection with the city government. These custodians of school moneys furnish a bond or other acceptable security for the protection of the school system. When the city chamberlain or treasurer is the custodian of school moneys his bond to the city covers the school funds handled by him.

Depositories

Inasmuch as New York is one of twenty-eight states in which the statutes provide for a local depository for local school funds,[3] it is not surprising to find that all the cities studied are using local depositories for school funds. There is some variation in the actual depositing of these funds, however. In the cities and villages having a separate school treasurer and in twelve of the cities in which the city treasurer or chamberlain is custodian of school funds, school moneys are deposited in accounts which are separate and distinct from other municipal accounts.[4] In six of these twelve cities the school tax is collected at a different time than is the city tax,[5] so that no administrative difficulties are encountered

[2] See Table XXVII, p. 87.
[3] Patty, W. W. "Legal Provisions for Custody of, and Liability for, Public Funds for Secondary School Support." *American School Board Journal*, Vol. 72, pp. 47, 48, 1926.
[4] See Table XXVII, p. 87.
[5] See Table XVI, p. 48.

TABLE XXVII

THE EXTENT TO WHICH SCHOOL FUNDS ARE KEPT
IN SEPARATE DEPOSITORY ACCOUNTS IN THE
THIRTY-FIVE CITIES IN WHICH THE CUSTODIAN OF
CITY FUNDS IS ALSO THE CUSTODIAN OF SCHOOL
FUNDS

	CITIES HAVING SEPARATE SCHOOL DEPOSITORY ACCOUNTS
Albany	
Amsterdam	
Auburn	x
Beacon	
Cohoes	
Dunkirk	
Elmira	
Fulton	
Glen Cove	x
Glens Falls	x
Gloversville	x
Hudson	
Jamestown	x
Johnstown	x
Lackawanna	x
Little Falls	
Lockport	
Mount Vernon	x*
New Rochelle	
Niagara Falls	
North Tonawanda	x
Oneida	
Oneonta	
Oswego	
Poughkeepsie	x
Rochester	x*
Rome	
Saratoga Springs	
Schenectady	
Syracuse	
Tonawanda	x*
Troy	
Utica	
Watervliet	
White Plains	
Total	12

* All school funds are not kept in this account.

in maintaining these separate depositories. In the other six
cities, school and city taxes are collected at the same time. In
three of these six, the custodian does not profess to keep all school
funds separate from city funds. The aim, however, is to keep

enough money in the school account at all times to meet all school needs. In the other three cities the custodian separates each day's collection into its component parts, depositing these amounts in their respective accounts. This procedure causes extra clerical work but it has its accompanying advantages.

Current Surpluses

Factors Creating Surpluses. In most types of private finance current expenditures are made from funds which are constantly being received for goods or for services rendered. Public finance, however, is quite different from private finance in this respect, in that it is largely dependent upon taxation for receipts with which to carry on its enterprises. Money from taxation could be collected weekly or monthly, but such procedure would not be practicable. Federal taxes are now payable quarterly, but most local taxes fall due annually or semi-annually. The comparatively small number of cities and villages in which school taxes are payable in two installments, or semi-annually, was shown earlier in this chapter.[6]

Whether school taxes are payable annually or semi-annually, special inducements are offered for the payment thereof within a short time after they become due and payable. These inducements vary in kind and amount. Some are positive inducements while others are negative. The inducement most frequently found in this study was the provision that taxes could be paid without penalty for a period of thirty days after they became due. Some cities offer a special inducement in the form of a discount if taxes are paid before a certain date, and still others add a small collection fee during a short period with a much larger fee thereafter. Regardless of the method pursued, these inducements operate to furnish to the school systems large sums of money before the need thereof arises. This is clearly brought out by Engelhardt and Engelhardt in their recent book on "Public School Business Administration."[7]

Since the existence of these balances is a product of the present tax collection machinery, it must be radically changed if these balances are to be materially reduced. It is doubtless impractical to collect taxes often enough to eliminate these balances entirely

---

[6] See Tables XXIII and XXIV, pp. 67 and 69.

[7] Engelhardt and Engelhardt. *Public School Business Administration,* Chap. XV, Bureau of Publications, Teachers College, Columbia University.

even if this were desirable. For this reason the author assumes that the present practice of having surpluses on hand during a part of the year at least will continue.

The economical administration of income requires that these balances be as productive as possible. Their productivity is dependent upon two factors; the alertness of those administering them, and interest rates. The first obligation of those administering these surpluses is to place them where they will earn the most interest before they are needed. The second obligation is to keep as large an amount as possible deposited in these places. In order to ascertain how well these surpluses were being administered in the cities studied, the writer investigated: first, the interest rate being paid by depositors for these funds; second, the possibilities of securing a greater return on present deposits; and third, the possibilities of depositing greater amounts at the maximum interest rate. These three aspects of the administration of current surpluses will be considered in turn.

Returns from Current Surpluses

Interest Rates. School funds are universally deposited in checking accounts in the local bank or banks of the cities visited. The rate of interest paid by the banks for the privilege of using these funds varies from zero per cent to 4.5 per cent as shown by Table XXVIII. In column 1 of this table appears the rate of interest which balances in checking accounts containing school moneys earned. In column 2 is shown the same information for general city balances as reported by the New York State Bureau of Municipal Information in a recent study.[8]

A comparison of these columns shows that city and school funds are earning the same returns in most of these cities. In a few cities school money is yielding no return while city money is, and vice versa. This situation is probably due to the inactivity of the respective officials therein.

Greater Returns from Deposits. Many banks will not pay interest on checking account balances unless some pressure is exerted by the depositor. This was verified by the writer time and again. In one city no effective pressure has been possible due to a charter provision that one-half of the city funds shall be deposited in each bank. When the school board in that city sold bonds re-

[8] *Municipal Bank Balances.* Report No. 133. Albany, N. Y. Dec. 4, 1927.

TABLE XXVIII

DATA ON THE FORTY-THREE CITIES STUDIED RELATIVE TO INTEREST RECEIVED ON DEPOSITORY BALANCES

CITIES	1 PER CENT RECEIVED ON SCHOOL CHECKING ACCOUNT BALANCES	2 PER CENT RECEIVED ON MUNICIPAL CHECKING ACCOUNT DAILY BALANCES +	3 SCHOOL ACCOUNT CREDITED WITH INTEREST ON BALANCES		4 MAINTAINS INACTIVE SCHOOL DEPOSITORY ACCOUNT	
			Yes	No	Yes(4)	No(4)
Albany	2	2		x		x
Amsterdam	3.6	3.6		x		x
Auburn	2	..*	x			x
Batavia	2	0	x			x
Beacon	2	2		x	x	
Canandaigua	0	2	x		x(3)	x
Cohoes	2	2		x		x
Corning	0	2		x		x
Dunkirk	1.5	1.5		x		x
Elmira	3.07	3.01	x			x
Fulton	2	..*		x		x
Geneva	0(1)	2		x		x
Glen Cove	2	2	x		x(5)	x
Glens Falls	4	4	x			x
Gloversville	0	0	x		x	
Hornell	3	2	x			x
Hudson	4.05	4.05		x		x
Jamestown	0	..*		x	x(6)	x
Johnstown	0	..*	x		x	
Lackawanna	4.5	..*	x			x
Little Falls	2	2		x		x
Lockport	2.5	2.5	x			x
Mechanicville	0	0	x		x	
Mount Vernon	2	1.875	x(2)			x
New Rochelle	2	2		x		x
Niagara Falls	2.5	..*		x		x
North Tonawanda	2	0	x		(x6)	
Norwich	0	0		x		x
Olean	2	2	x		x(7)	x
Oneida	2.5	2		x		x
Oneonta	2	2		x		x
Oswego	0	0		x		x
Poughkeepsie	3.0	3.0	x			x
Rochester	1.5	1.5	x(2)			x
Rome	2	2		x	x	
Saratoga Springs	0	0	x(6)		x(6)	x
Schenectady	0	3		x		x
Syracuse	3.5	..*		x		x
Tonawanda	2	2	x(2)			x
Troy	2	2		x		x
Utica	4.41	4.41		x		x
Watervliet	2	2		x		x
White Plains	2	2		x		x
Totals	43	36	19	24	11	37

+See footnote 8, p. 89, for source of data.
* Not included in report.
(1) Bank has paid interest in past.
(2) Interest on some school money goes to city.
(3) Small sinking or surplus fund.
(4) Current school funds unless stated otherwise.
(5) Insurance adjustment funds.
(6) Building funds.
(7) Funds from early sale of bonds.

cently, these banks were willing to pay for the use of the moneys therefrom when they were assured that they could not have the use of them otherwise. In another city in which no return was being received from school deposits while city money was yielding a return, the city chamberlain assured the writer that no interest had been paid by the banks for city money until pressure had been exerted.

One method of securing a maximum return on deposits is to patronize that bank which will pay the highest interest rate. This bank is chosen after bids have been submitted by those banks which desire the use of these moneys. In only seven cities was this method being practiced, but in these cities the interest rate was well above that being received on similar deposits in the other cities.

Popular demand is another method of securing a larger return on deposits. If local bankers are made to feel that they are not paying as much for these funds as they should, nor as much as are banks in comparable communities, a higher interest rate will often be paid. For this reason wide publicity should be given local and foreign interest rates. There is no justification in permitting local bankers to thrive on free use of public moneys.

Many of the school systems visited are not getting the interest earned by school moneys. Column 3, Table XXVIII, page 90, shows that in only nineteen of these forty-three cities does the school system receive this interest. In the remaining twenty-four cities any interest earned by these funds augments the general city fund. Some school boards have been able to secure this interest after debating the issue with municipal officials. Some are now engaged in such a campaign. Legal opinion seems to favor the school board in this matter, but in the absence of any court decision it seems to remain in the controversial stage.

Another possibility in the administration of surpluses so that a larger return may be received therefrom is to deposit such funds in inactive or savings accounts. Reference to column 4, Table XXVIII, page 90, makes clear that this possibility has not been fully realized in these cities. In only eleven cities does the custodian of school moneys take advantage of the larger interest rates which are paid on funds deposited in inactive accounts, and in three of these the school system receives no benefit therefrom.[9]

[9] See column 3, Table XXVIII, p. 90.

Of the other eight, only three are so administering current funds that a part thereof yields a return to the school systems before it must be used to meet school needs. In these three cities, Gloversville, Johnstown, and Mechanicville, no interest is received on balances in the checking accounts. This is also true in many cities which do not deposit surplus moneys in inactive accounts.

Larger Amounts on Deposit. A third check on the economical administration of surpluses remains to be considered. It concerns the possibilities of depositing greater amounts at the maximum interest rate than is now being done. It has just been shown that very few school systems are depositing funds in inactive or savings accounts. Perhaps available balances do not permit such a practice. In order to ascertain whether this was true or not, the writer discovered the extent to which monthly balances were being carried in the cities and villages of this study.

It was not possible to discover monthly balances in some of the school systems visited. It is obvious that these could not be ascertained for the school systems in which city and school funds are deposited together. In other school systems accounts were so kept that these balances were not obtainable in the time at the writer's disposal. These data, however, were secured in seventeen cities and villages. Monthly balances over a period of at least two years were secured. Space does not permit the inclusion of such data from all these seventeen cities, but a sufficient number of typical cities will be shown to give a true picture of the data secured.

Of the seventeen school systems in which complete data on monthly balances were available, there were four in which a portion of the funds was being deposited in inactive accounts until needed, thereby enabling the school system to secure greater returns. Tables XXIX and XXX reveal the details of the administration of these balances in two of these cities. In neither of these cities could this administration be considered ideal, but they illustrate what can be done along this line.

The village supplying the data shown in Table XXIX began the present economical administration of its cash balances in January, 1924. This village is unique in that its school board is depositing funds in a neighboring city bank. The local bank would pay no interest on checking account balances, so all available funds were taken to a neighboring city bank which was willing to pay

TABLE XXIX

BALANCE IN THE SCHOOL FUNDS IN VILLAGE A AT THE END OF EACH
MONTH DURING TWO SCHOOL FISCAL YEARS, TOGETHER WITH THE PARTS
OF THAT BALANCE WHICH WERE IN THE TWO DEPOSITORIES

	1	2	3
MONTH		1924–1925	
	* BALANCE AT THE END OF THE MONTH	DEPOSITED IN NEIGHBORING CITY BANK AT 4 PER CENT INTEREST	BALANCE IN LOCAL BANK. NO INTEREST
August	$ 7,807.55	$ ..	$ 7,807.55
September	4,681.46	..	4,681.46
October	71,826.21	..	71,826.21
November	64,054.42	..	64,054.42
December	54,435.29	48,886.14	5,549.15
January	43,080.18	42,442.90	637.28
February	59,612.20	59,124.25	487.95
March	306,580.81	292,751.20	13,829.61
April	294,034.19	290,713.58	3,320.61
May	279,346.16	269,056.71	10,289.45
June	246,803.25	239,012.28	7,790.97
July	213,834.73	212,725.71	1,109.02

* Total Expenditures During the Year $239,126.16

MONTH	1925–1926		
August	$ 699.15	$ 84.01	$ 615.14
September	13,423.68	84.29	13,339.39
October	83,059.59	80,261.04	2,798.55
November	73,298.36	71,513.88	1,784.48
December	60,596.11	59,729.14	866.97
January	49,103.55	47,881.76	1,221.79
February	36,178.45	34,001.46	2,176.99
March	17,700.68	16,091.98	1,608.70
April	18,511.52	9,131.85	9,379.67
May	21,590.70	9,162.89	12,427.81
June	4,413.48	2,122.21	2,291.27
July	1,540.81	..	1,540.81

* Total Expenditures During the Year $171,241.77

4 per cent interest upon them with checking privileges. Only
enough money is kept in the local bank to meet current bills,
amounts being transferred thereto from the interest-paying bank
periodically.

TABLE XXX

BALANCE IN THE SCHOOL FUND IN CITY B AT THE END OF EACH MONTH
DURING TWO SCHOOL FISCAL YEARS, TOGETHER WITH THE PARTS OF
THAT BALANCE WHICH WERE IN THE TWO DEPOSITORIES

	1	2	3
MONTH	1924–1925		
	* BALANCE AT THE END OF THE MONTH	BALANCE IN SPECIAL FUND EARNING 4 PER CENT	BALANCE IN CHECKING ACCOUNT EARNING 2 PER CENT
August	$249,379.24	$242,467.16	$ 6,912.08
September	316,119.20	232,551.32	83,567.88
October	386,271.67	232,638.56	153,633.11
November	334,838.59	232,723.20	102,115.39
December	296,618.83	237,148.88	59,469.95
January	262,077.12	237,955.70	24,121.42
February	252,946.39	238,686.65	14,259.74
March	218,407.12	209,485.66	8,921.46
April	537,323.93	533,586.19	3,737.74
May	497,632.78	475,272.31	22,360.47
June	473,871.95	456,789.90	17,082.05
July	435,877.68	433,303.46	2,574.22

* Total Expenditures During the Year $480,951.75

MONTH	1925–1926		
August	$382,110.10	$374,663.72	$ 7,446.38
September	434,525.97	360,874.79	73,651.18
October	485,071.94	362,097.31	122,974.63
November	420,189.41	363,289.39	56,900.02
December	353,012.01	339,498.02	13,513.99
January	306,667.70	295,594.62	11,073.08
February	252,718.46	246,451.81	6,266.65
March	190,812.82	187,232.06	3,580.76
April	151,153.10	142,731.65	8,421.45
May	207,224.17	204,923.70	2,300.47
June	157,740.91	149,334.61	8,406.30
July	126,120.05	122,975.43	3,144.62

* Total Expenditures During the Year $731,342.44

The city shown in Table XXX maintains a special inactive fund
in a local depository. It has not kept its checking account as
small as could be economically justified, especially during the
early months of the fiscal year. This school board, however, is
making an attempt at an economical administration of surplus

funds. It was able to maintain smaller balances in the checking account during the second year for which data are shown than during the first year, and will doubtless continue to improve its administration of these balances as further experience is gained.

TABLE XXXI

BALANCE IN THE SCHOOL FUND IN CITY C AT THE END OF EACH MONTH
DURING THREE SCHOOL FISCAL YEARS

MONTH	BALANCE AT THE END OF THE MONTH		
	1923–1924	1924–1925	1925–1926
August	$ 128.15	$ 85.48	$ 8,290.37
September	617.33	30.02	6,682.87
October	23,612.74	41,033.52	44,485.27
November	45,332.53	49,282.45	51,219.57
December	31,375.57	43,789.94	46,128.06
January	30,856.77	36,099.51	36,893.83
February	20,189.20	27,846.93	27,853.14
March	12,075.35	29,250.79	20,807.88
April	14,689.84	20,742.74	21,816.07
May	5,323.36	21,209.60	21,600.88
June	3,418.55	11,422.14	13,453.58
July	1,789.06	10,017.08	11,858.42
Total Expenditures ..	$136,304.06	$133,165.04	$131,442.50

TABLE XXXII

BALANCE IN THE SCHOOL FUND IN CITY D AT THE END OF EACH MONTH
DURING THREE SCHOOL FISCAL YEARS

MONTH	BALANCE AT THE END OF THE MONTH		
	1923–1924	1924–1925	1925–1926
August	$ 36,949.17	$ 24,252.85	$ 22,955.13
September	19,829.49	44,262.93	2,673.79
October	19,785.74	228,840.01	14,704.86
November	127,261.74	195,455.68	187,696.12
December	120,506.61	173,508.68	185,499.60
January	103,776.62	159,720.75	167,469.40
February	81,441.16	134,478.48	143,188.86
March	77,299.88	138,644.83	107,827.73
April	59,248.44	68,735.70	73,184.45
May	62,280.81	68,794.87	75,452.70
June	34,972.15	31,626.96	52,817.21
July	28,227.89	26,993.19	47,791.47
Total Expenditures ..	$242,089.21	$328,318.54	$339,245.78

TABLE XXXIII

BALANCE IN THE SCHOOL FUND IN CITY E AT THE END OF EACH MONTH
DURING THREE SCHOOL FISCAL YEARS

MONTH	BALANCE AT THE END OF THE MONTH		
	1924	1925	1926
January	$268,043.78	$172,513.26	$188,994.83
February	277,110.61	234,237.16	214,310.93
March	260,709.78	220,562.29	202,424.72
April	289,187.33	228,823.79	205,926.16
May	164,434.88	225,715.97	198,710.94
June	149,438.84	210,733.32	170,545.25
July	142,860.34	202,629.25	158,873.49
August	127,996.28	190,185.49	142,448.40
September	104,943.22	154,890.55	106,450.06
October	78,983.89	124,899.06	67,572.73
November	49,014.55	84,019.42	44,144.66
December	26,223.74	61,663.08	5,727.16
Total Expenditures ..	$436,809.48	$411,001.87	$441,839.70

TABLE XXXIV

BALANCE IN THE SCHOOL FUND IN CITY F AT THE END OF EACH MONTH
DURING THREE SCHOOL FISCAL YEARS

MONTH	BALANCE AT THE END OF THE MONTH		
	1924	1925	1926
January	$ 6,478.11	$216,404.69	$181,195.12
February	16,446.30	60,032.55	343,018.94
March	260,913.83	98,925.78	227,246.59
April	221,305.91	64,428.34	192,444.92
May	106,738.30	357,652.49	319,344.53
June	73,616.14	237,712.08	113,291.83
July	158,425.58	115,794.81	286,787.46
August	93,672.08	74,315.75	214,312.51
September	189,357.95	387,728.02	247,153.40
October	89,239.64	282,190.60	150,672.02
November	195,082.55	152,461.71	28,921.74
December	98,818.69	129,621.95	74,887.51
Total Expenditures ..	$1,275,194.50	$1,431,922.34	$1,623,712.66

The data contained in Tables XXXI to XXXIV inclusive are typical of the data found in the other cities. An examination of the monthly balances over a period of three years in these cities shows a striking similarity between those amounts from year to year. In every case, as is true in those cities not shown, comparatively large amounts could be placed in savings accounts for periods ranging from six to twelve months, as is being done in several cities of which those in Tables XXIX and XXX are typical. By making an analysis similar to that made in these cities, each city should discover the amount which it could safely deposit in an inactive account for the purpose of receiving therefrom a greater return.

This is a period wherein the call for retrenchment in school expenditures is being heard on every hand. Economy and sound business procedures should be universal in the administration of public school moneys. This study has revealed numerous possibilities for further economy in such administration in the cities and villages studied. It is hoped that the disclosures and the recommendations herein contained will be valuable not only to the cities studied but to other cities as well.

Summary

In the cities of this study in which school taxes are being collected after these funds are needed, four types of adjustment designed to meet these needs are being made. These adjustments, stated in the order of greatest frequency encountered, are: (1) the advancement of money from the general city fund with which to meet school needs; (2) negotiation for short-term loans by the school board in anticipation of taxes; (3) surplus revenue funds with which to meet school needs previous to the collection of taxes; and (4) delaying payment of bills until tax moneys are received. Each of these adjustments would be unnecessary if the tax calendar were properly coördinated with the fiscal year. The necessity for these adjustments is decreasing since many cities either have advanced or are in the process of advancing the date when school taxes are due.

The present method of tax collection in the cities and villages of this study makes relatively large amounts of school money available before it is needed. In the interest of the taxpayers who make this money available, the school board is morally and legally bound to administer it economically and safely.

In thirty-five of the forty-three cities studied, the custodian of city funds is also custodian of school funds. In twelve of these thirty-five cities and in all school systems having a separate school treasurer, school funds are deposited in accounts separate and distinct from municipal funds. This separation of funds is highly desirable, for temptation to make use of these funds for other purposes is thereby lessened. This separation also permits the school fund to profit by the interest which these funds earn before they are needed. This is seldom true when city and school funds are deposited together.

The interest rates paid by depositories for the use of school funds are practically the same as are being paid for the use of city funds. These rates vary greatly from city to city. The highest rates are paid in cities where the depository is chosen after bids for the use of these funds have been submitted. This method of selecting the depository should be followed more extensively than is now the case. Interest rates can often be increased by pressure of public opinion. School boards should make every legitimate effort to secure an increase in the rate of interest received on deposits.

The school boards of the state are not depositing their funds in savings accounts as extensively as balances on hand during the year warrant. Since the rate of interest paid for the use of funds deposited in such accounts is often nearly twice that paid on checking account balances, it is evident that a maximum amount should be kept in such accounts at all times. A careful analysis of past monthly balances will enable the custodian of school moneys to ascertain the amount which can be so deposited in order that a maximum return on current surpluses will be assured. Careful planning in this phase of income control will yield large dividends to the school system and therefore to the taxpayers.

CHAPTER VI

RECAPITULATIONS

In the preceding chapters certain phases of income control as they are operating in the cities and villages of New York State have been presented. Following the consideration of each such phase a summary of findings and recommendations has been given. The purpose of this chapter is to bring together the most significant of the findings and recommendations of this study.

The Tax Calendar and the Fiscal Year

The most significant findings in this study were those which resulted from a study of the events in the tax calendar as their occurrence affected the availability of money when needed by the school systems. Moneys from local taxation still constitute a large proportion of the funds available for the public schools in the cities and villages of New York State. Obviously, if these tax moneys fail to appear when the need for them arises some adjustment must be made. Sound business procedure demands that the tax assessing and collecting machinery be properly coördinated with the disbursing machinery. This coördination can be secured by so arranging the tax calendar that taxes will be collected early in the fiscal year, preferably beginning tax collection with the opening of the new fiscal year.

This ideal is far from realization in the cities studied. In one of these cities school taxes were collected as early as eighty-nine days *before*, and in one as late as two hundred twenty days *after* the beginning of the fiscal year. There is certainly no valid reason why taxes should be collected three months before the beginning of the year during which such moneys are to be spent, and sound financial procedure forbids that tax collection be delayed for over seven months after the beginning of the then current year. Of the forty-three cities and seven villages included in this study, school tax collection began before the first month of the fiscal year had passed in twenty-two cities and one village,

while in twenty-one cities and six villages it did not begin until
after the first month had elapsed.

Factors Delaying Tax Collection

A careful study of the tax calendar in these two almost equal
groups of cities revealed that the completion of the assessment
roll and the final approval of the school budget by the reviewing
authority were the two events which operated to delay tax collection.

In the first group of cities referred to above, the assessment
roll was completed thirteen days before the budget was adopted
by the local school board in the median city of that group and
34.8 days before it was approved by the reviewing authority.
In the median city of the second group of cities the assessment
roll was not completed until fifty-six days after the budget had
been adopted by the local board and thirty-two days after it had
been approved by the reviewing authority. In only eighteen of
the fifty cities and villages studied was the assessment roll completed before the school budget was adopted by the board of
education, and in only twenty-seven did the reviewing authorities
know the assessed valuation for taxing purposes when they put
their stamp of approval upon the school budget. In eighteen of
the twenty-seven cities and villages wherein school tax collection
began the second month of the fiscal year or later, the assessment
roll was not completed until after the opening of the fiscal year.
In one city it was not completed until half of the new fiscal year
had passed, and in ten cities its completion dated later than the
first month of that year.

In light of these data it is obvious that the cities of the second
group must revise their assessing machinery so as to guarantee
a completed assessment roll earlier in the fiscal year if tax collection is to begin early enough to meet financial needs. In order
to begin tax collection near the beginning of the fiscal year, the
completed assessment roll should be available at least two weeks
before the fiscal year begins. This will be possible if proper attention is paid to this event in the tax calendar.

Budgetary Review

While, as was shown in Chapter I, only a small percentage of
the school boards in the cities of New York State are fiscally

dependent upon municipal officials, it is still necessary to submit the school budget for review in a large percentage of these cities. In the cities visited only seven school boards are fiscally dependent, but in all but four of these forty-three cities the school boards must submit their budgets for review after those bodies of informed laymen have determined the needs of the schools for the year in question. In many instances these reviewing authorities can have no final voice in determining the amount carried by the budget, but legislative red tape still requires that it be presented for review. It was found that this requirement necessitated a delay in beginning tax collection with little or no gain to offset the extra expense incurred by late tax collection.

It was found that considerable time elapsed between the date of adoption of the budget by the school board and the date of its approval by the final reviewing authority. In one city one hundred thirty-eight days elapsed between these two dates. This was an extreme case, but in twelve cities this time span was as long as forty-five days. Reviewing authorities in cities whose school fiscal year begins January 1 took a longer time on the average than did the reviewing authorities in cities whose school fiscal year begins August 1. While the writer sees no justification for requiring that the school budget be formally reviewed by municipal authorities, so long as it is required by law, steps should be taken to guarantee early action by the reviewing authority to the end that tax collection need not be unduly late in the fiscal year.

Collection of taxes late in the fiscal year was not caused by failure of school boards to adopt their school estimates, for it was found that regardless of the size of the city, school tax collection late in the school fiscal year was not made necessary by delay in adopting the budget on the part of the local school boards.

Submission of the Budget for Review

It was found that in many cities the school budget was required to be submitted to the reviewing authorities by the school board far in advance of the fiscal year. In one city this was required nearly eight months before the fiscal year was to begin. Based upon a careful analysis of when the events in the tax calendar of the several cities of this study occurred and the assumption that the present external income controls will continue, the writer concluded that, if the budget is submitted for review between sixty and ninety days prior to the beginning of the school fiscal year, sufficient time will be provided for the occurrence of all events incident to the collection of school taxes at the beginning of the fiscal year. This conclusion is in harmony with recommendations of authorities in municipal finance.

In nine of the cities and all of the villages of this study the budget after adoption by the school board must be approved by the legal voters. This election is usually held nearly three months before the fiscal year begins. This requirement forces the adoption of the budget before adequate data upon which to base it are available. The writer, therefore, recommends that the law requiring the annual school meeting on the first Tuesday in May be modified to permit this meeting late in July or early in August, at which time the assessment roll should be complete so that school tax collection can be started without delay.

Cities in Which the Tax Calendar Has Been Coördinated with the School Fiscal Year

A number of cities were discovered in which the tax calendar .was well coördinated with the fiscal year. In an effort to ascertain the conditioning factors in such coördination, these cities were grouped according to a number of criteria. Of all these groupings only one seemed significant. The criterion satisfied by that group of cities was the simultaneous collection of school, state, county, and city taxes.[1] Further analysis of the fourteen cities satisfying this criterion revealed several other common elements. From this analysis it was found that twelve of these fourteen cities began the collection of taxes within .the first month of the fiscal year; in thirteen of these cities the school fiscal year begins January 1; in twelve of these cities the school budget received final approval before the fiscal year began; in every city of this group the assessed valuations for the following tax year were known before the school budgets for the corresponding year received final approval and in advance of the beginning of the school fiscal year; in all of these cities the school and municipal fiscal year coincide; and in thirteen of them city and school taxes are payable in two semi-annual installments usually without fee for this privilege.

[1] For the cities in this group see Table XXIV, p. 69.

It was gratifying to discover that a number of cities have recently taken the necessary steps to advance the dates of the events in the tax calendar so that taxes can be collected nearer the beginning of the fiscal year. Cities in which the tax calendar is becoming more nearly coördinated with the school fiscal year include Jamestown, Rochester, Syracuse, and Schenectady. Other cities should follow the example of these and the other cities which have arranged this coördination.

Collection of Taxes

There should be but one tax receiver in a city or village. This official will tend to be a municipal employee, but the school board should stand its proportionate share of the expense of this office, especially if this board is fiscally independent. This is not universally done in the cities studied although in all but four of these forty-three cities the school tax is being collected by a municipal employee. In the villages this tax is usually collected by a school tax collector who is not associated with the village government. In Westchester and Nassau counties school taxes are collected by the receiver of taxes for the town in which the village is situated.

In seventeen of the cities and five of the villages studied, school taxes are collected when no other tax is being paid. This procedure is advantageous in that the taxpayer then knows what he is paying for schools. In eight cities school taxes are collected at the same time as city taxes; in four cities and two villages, school, state, and county taxes are collected together; and in fourteen cities, school, state, county, and city taxes are collected at the same time. The last combination seems to favor administrative adjustments, for these fourteen cities have numerous desirable practices in common as shown above.

Collection of the various kinds of taxes should, as far as practicable, be so timed that the burden of their payment will be distributed throughout the year. Efforts to meet this criterion have apparently caused delay in the collection of school taxes, but this has usually been due to the fact that the date for the collection of city taxes has not been properly coördinated with the municipal fiscal year. In those cities whose school and municipal fiscal years begin January 1, the most satisfactory solution of these problems has been the collection of all taxes together in two approximately equal installments in January and July. In those cities in which the municipal fiscal year begins January 1, and the school fiscal year on August 1, the city taxes should be collected in January and the school taxes in August. By so doing the above criterion would be met.

Fiscal Year Dates

Theoretically, the most desirable date for the beginning of the school fiscal year is July 1. Actually, something over half of the school systems in the cities of the United States have adopted this date. Of the forty-three cities and seven villages included in this study, only one, a village, has chosen this date; twenty cities and six villages have fiscal years beginning August 1; the fiscal year in twenty-two cities begins January 1, and in one, April 1. Since a number of the analyses in this study were made of cities grouped according to these school fiscal year dates, a summary of the findings is given here.

In meeting the legal requirements which prescribe the dates when the school boards shall submit their budgets to the municipal officials for review, the cities whose school fiscal year begins January 1 do not measure up to the cities and villages whose school fiscal year begins August 1. In the former group of cities, more school boards failed to adopt their budget estimates by the dates prescribed for their submission to the reviewing authority than was the case in the group whose school fiscal year begins August 1. The school board in the median city of the former group adopted its estimate 3.7 days before the date set for its submission for review, while in the median city of the latter group it was adopted 8.5 days before that date. The school estimate was adopted by the school board after the date set for its submission for review in over twice as many of the cities in the former group as in the latter.

In the cities whose school fiscal year begins January 1, a much greater time was taken by the municipal authorities to review the school budget than was taken by the corresponding officials in the cities whose school fiscal year begins August 1. In the median city of the former group forty-one days were taken up with this review, while in the median city of the latter group only 11.5 days were required. The greater lapse of time in performing this function in cities whose school fiscal year begins January 1 was doubtless due to the many duties which confronted the municipal officials at the time the school budget was submitted for review. In all but four of these cities the school tax is collected at the same time as the general city tax, which means that all other departmental estimates are being considered at the same time as the school estimate. The final approval of the school budget, although satisfactory as to amount, is often delayed because of its being considered an integral part of the general city budget. In only three cities whose school fiscal year begins August 1 is the school budget in this way dependent upon the general city budget.

The total length of time which elapsed from the date when the budget was adopted by the school board until the date when it was approved by the final reviewing authority was dependent upon neither the size of the city nor the type of external control exercised over school income.

The groups of cities whose school fiscal year begins January 1 and August 1, respectively, have reached about the same stage in the adjustment of their tax calendars with their school fiscal years. A somewhat larger percentage of the cities in the former group began tax collection during the first month of the fiscal year, but in a slightly larger percentage of those in the latter group tax collection began within one month after major expenditures had to be made. From a financial standpoint the latter measure is the more valid, so there is a slight advantage favoring the cities whose fiscal year begins August 1 in this respect.

The above findings do not conclusively prove the superiority of either set of fiscal year dates over the other one. In each case the cities whose school fiscal year begins August 1 have made the best showing, but the margin in each case has been slight. Theoretically, this date is the more desirable for it coincides with the academic year which is the administrative year for which contractual obligations are made. It is also the legal reporting year to the State Department of Education.

The present type of external income control in many of these school systems requires that the school fiscal year begin January 1, due to the fact that the municipal fiscal year begins at that time; but when this control is changed the school fiscal year should be made to coincide with the school reporting year. Something should be done more nearly to harmonize the many existing fiscal year dates in state and municipal government. The trend in some quarters is toward acceptance of the calendar year as the fiscal year. A universal acceptance of this or some other period would greatly simplify the many financial analyses which are now being made.

INTERNAL INCOME CONTROL

Teachers' Retirement Fund

The analysis of budgetary procedure in the cities of this study revealed deficiencies and unsound practices in providing for payments and deductions for the Teachers' Retirement Fund. In sixteen of these cities and in three villages the budget is being padded by the procedures now practiced. The manner in which the State Retirement Board administers payments to this fund through the Statistical Bureau of the State Department of Education creates the confusion which accompanies the unsound practices revealed in Chapter III. By these practices the school boards are asking for more money from local taxation than would be necessary to balance their budgets if they were properly prepared. Sample budgets illustrating the sound and unsound methods being followed were also given in Chapter III.

Budgetary procedure would be simplified by a change in the method of making payments to the Retirement Fund. The most desirable method from the standpoint of the men in the field would be the payment of these contributions direct to the Retirement Board by the administrative units monthly, or annually if monthly payments would cause too great a clerical expense in the office of the Retirement Board.

Capital Outlay and Debt Service

In fourteen of the forty-three cities, and in one of the seven villages studied, expenditures for capital outlay, for debt service, or for both, are not included in the school budget by the school board. These services are provided by the municipal government in these cities. This procedure often leaves the citizens uninformed concerning the total cost of education to the community. It is an accepted principle of school administration that the school authorities should have complete authority over the entire school budget. This establishes a direct responsibility for all school expenditures and is far superior to the divided responsibility found in these fourteen cities.

Administrative Control of Income

Custodian of School Funds

In thirty-five of the forty-three cities studied the custodian of municipal funds is also the custodian of school funds. This is desirable if school funds are kept separate from municipal funds. In only twelve of these cities were school funds actually deposited in accounts separate and distinct from municipal accounts. This separation is highly desirable and should be universal, for temptation to make use of these funds for other than school purposes is thereby lessened. This separation also permits the school fund to profit by the interest earned by these funds. This return is seldom realized when school and city funds are deposited together.

Interest on Balances

The interest rates paid by depositories for the use of school moneys are practically the same as are being paid for the use of city funds, with notable exceptions. The highest rates are paid in cities where the depository is chosen after bids for the use of these funds have been submitted. This method of selecting the depository should be followed more extensively than is now being done. Interest rates can often be increased by pressure of public opinion. School boards should make every legitimate effort to secure an increase in the rate of interest received on deposits.

The school boards of the state are not depositing their funds in savings or other inactive accounts as extensively as balances on hand during the year would warrant. Since the rate of interest paid for the use of money deposited in such accounts is often nearly twice that paid on checking account balances, it is evident that a maximum amount should be kept in such accounts at all times. A careful analysis of past monthly balances will enable the custodian of school funds to ascertain the amount which can be deposited in order that a maximum return on current surpluses may be assured before they are needed to meet future obligations.

BIBLIOGRAPHY

ALEXANDER, CARTER. *Bibliography on Educational Finance.* The Macmillan Company, 1924. 257 pp.

ALLEN, R. F. *Special Statutes and Provisions of Charters in the Several Cities of New York State,* 1921. (Unpublished report on file in the Legal Division, State Department of Education, Albany, N. Y.)

BAKER, G. M. "Financial Practices in Cities and Towns Below 25,000," *American School Board Journal,* Vol. 53, p. 20, Dec. 1916.

BUCK, A. E. *Budget Making.* Appendix IV, p. 219. D. Appleton and Company, 1921. 234 pp.

BUCK, A. E. *Municipal Budgets and Budget Making,* p. 37. New York City, National Municipal League, 1925. (Out of print.)

CASE, H. C. "Uniform Systems for Recording Disbursements for School Purposes as Prescribed for New York State." *American School Board Journal,* Vol. 53, pp. 24–26, 68, Oct. 1916.

CLEVELAND, F. A. *Chapters on Municipal Administration and Accounting,* pp. 62 ff. Longmans, Green & Co., 1909. 361 pp.

CUBBERLEY, E. P. *Public School Administration,* pp. 104–05. Houghton Mifflin Company. 1922. 479 pp.

DALEY, R. L. "School Accounting Officers and Relations to the Preparation of the Budget." *Fourteenth Annual Proceedings, National Association of Public School Business Officials,* 1925. p. 66.

DEFFENBAUGH, W. S. *Current Practice in City School Administration.* U. S. Govt. Report, Department of Interior (Bureau of Education Bulletin, 1917, No. 8). pp. 32 ff. 98 pp.

ENGELHARDT, N. L. and ENGELHARDT, FRED. "Administrative and Accounting Control of Income in Local School Systems." *Teachers College Record,* Vol. XXVIII, No. 3, pp. 272 ff. Nov. 1926.

ENGELHARDT, N. L. and ENGELHARDT, FRED. "Budgetary Practices in Local School Systems." *Teachers College Record,* Vol. XXVIII, No. 4. pp. 394–412. Dec. 1926.

ENGELHARDT, N. L. and ENGELHARDT, FRED. *Public School Business Administration.* Bureau of Publications, Teachers College, Columbia University, 1927. pp. 308 ff; pp. 508 ff. 1068 pp.

FOWLKES, J. G. *The Accounting of Public School Expenditures in Wisconsin.* Bureau of Educational Research, Bulletin No. 4, University of Wisconsin, 1924. 60 pp.

Frasier, George W. *Control of City School Finances.* The Bruce Publishing Company, 1922. 132 pp.

Gilbert, Frank B. "Some Legal Aspects of the City School Problem." Reprint, *Journal of New York State Teachers Association,* Jan. 1924. 11 pp.

Gilbert, Frank B. *Extracts from Memorandum on Senate Bill.* Printed Number 425, Feb. 23, 1921.

Henzlik, Frank E. *Rights and Liabilities of Public School Boards Under Capital Outlay Contracts.* Bureau of Publications, Teachers College, Columbia University, 1924. 118 pp.

Hutchinson, J. H. *School Costs and School Accounting.* Contributions to Education, No. 62. Bureau of Publications, Teachers College, Columbia University, 1914. 151 pp.

McGaughy, J. R. *The Fiscal Administration of City School Systems.* The Macmillan Company, 1924. 95 pp.

Moehlman, A. E. *Public School Finance,* pp. 172–186, 200–211, 229–281. Rand, McNally & Company, 1927. 508 pp.

Morehart, G. C. *The Legal Status of City School Boards.* Bureau of Publications, Teachers College, Columbia University, 1927.

Morrison, J. Cayce. *The Legal Status of the City School Superintendent.* Warwick and York, Incorporated, 1922. 162 pp.

New York State Bureau of Municipal Information. *Municipal Bank Balances.* Report No. 133, Dec. 4, 1927. Albany, N. Y. (Typewritten.)

New York State Bureau of Municipal Information. *How and When Taxes are Collected in New York State Cities.* Report No. 303, Dec. 14, 1917. Albany, N. Y. (Typewritten.)

New York State Tax Commission, 1925 Report of, Legislative Document (1926), No. 7. pp. 119 ff. Albany, J. B. Lyon Company, 471 pp.

Patty, W. W. "Legal Provisions for Custody of, and Liability for, Public Funds for Secondary School Support." *American School Board Journal,* Vol. 72, pp. 47–48. March, 1926.

Pennsylvania School Laws. Sections 523, 524, 527, 537, 549, and 561. Harrisburg, 1923.

Pittenger, B. F. *An Introduction to Public School Finance,* pp. 45–72. Houghton Mifflin Company, 1925. 372 pp.

Rollins, Frank. *School Administration in Municipal Government.* Columbia University Contributions to Philosophy, Vol. II, pp. 24 ff. The Macmillan Company, 1902. 106 pp.

Smith, H. P. *Business Administration of a City School System.* Contributions to Education, No. 197. Bureau of Publications, Teachers College, Columbia University, 1925. 129 pp.

Special Joint Committee on Taxation and Retrenchment, Report of, Retrenchment Section Legislative Document No. 80. pp. 19–20. Albany, J. B. Lyon Company, 1920. 155 pp.

Special Joint Committee on Taxation and Retrenchment, Report of, Legislative Document No. 97, p. 19. Albany, J. B. Lyon Company, 1925. 259 pp.

STRAYER, G. D. and ENGELHARDT, N. L.   *The Classroom Teacher,* pp. 28–29. American Book Company, 1920. 400 pp.

STRAYER, G. D. and HAIG, R. M.   *The Financing of Education in the State of New York.* The Macmillan Company, 1923. 205 pp.

Survey of the Government, Finance, and Administration of Newark, N. J. Part I; N. Y. Bureau of Municipal Research. Nov. 1919.

TRUSLER, HARRY R.   "Illegal Expenditures of School Money." *American School Board Journal,* Vol. 50, pp. 19–20, 78.   Feb. 1915; Vol. 50, pp. 18–19, 65, March, 1915.